Taking Ownership of Your Career

Taking Ownership of Your Career

David D. Van Fleet

BEP
BUSINESS EXPERT PRESS
Leader in applied, concise business books

Taking Ownership of Your Career

First published in 2025 by
Business Expert Press, LLC
222 East 46th Street, New York, NY 10017
www.businessexpertpress.com

ISBN-13: 978-1-63742-894-8 (paperback)
ISBN-13: 978-1-63742-895-5 (e-book)

Business Career Development Collection

First edition: 2025

10 9 8 7 6 5 4 3 2 1

EU SAFETY REPRESENTATIVE
Mare Nostrum Group B.V.
Mauritskade 21D
1091 GC Amsterdam
The Netherlands
gpsr@mare-nostrum.co.uk

Contents

List of Tables

Tables

Review Quotes

"*Empowering individuals is crucial to organizations. This book provides broadly comprehensive and immediately applicable look at the ways individuals can be empowered. The novel use of the V-REEL® Framework to focus on explaining this really makes it all understandable and relevant. I think that David Van Fleet's unique perspective will serve to improve team interactions, performance, and outcomes. I, for one, see this book as a significant contribution to organizational effectiveness.*"—**Felix P. Nater, President and Owner of Nater Associates, Ltd. (A human resource security management consulting practice focusing on workplace violence and security consulting)**

"*This lucid, insightful, and comprehensive monograph is a 'must-read' for managers who wish to understand and extirpate dysfunctional behavior in organizations. Although written by the world's leading scholar on this topic, it presents 'lessons learned' in a user-friendly format. An instant classic.*"—**Donald Siegel, Foundation Professor and Co-Executive Director, Global Center for Technology Transfer, School of Public Affairs, Arizona State University**

Preface

Studies into workplace violence, terrorism, and other forms of dysfunctional behavior associated with work suggested to us that there was a need for a book that would not only educate others on these topics but also help those who wanted to reduce their risks by choosing relatively safe jobs.

No job is completely safe. You can get paper cuts, be injured by a staple, or cut yourself with a letter opener. You can slip, trip, stumble, and fall. You can sit or stand in one position too long. You could get fired even though you are performing well. You can be a victim of sabotage or harassment, sometimes because you are doing an outstanding job. There are simply a lot of ways to get hurt—physically or emotionally—on the job.

However, you can evaluate the potential risk or relative safety of a job before you make a career decision. You can learn things to look for that will enable you to make a more rational, informed decision about a potential job or work site.

This book is designed to help you do just that. I wish you luck in your job hunting and in your job.

Description

This book can be valuable to a single reader but even more valuable if used in a group or classroom setting where concepts and reactions can be discussed and debated. Each chapter asks you to think about the material and what you learned in the chapter and provides an anecdote example. There is also a glossary and an extensive reading list to assist in further exploring finding a safe job.

Standards

This book has six standards to ensure its value to you, the reader: being readable, being interesting, being up-to-date, being accurate, being unique, and audience. The first two ensure that the content remains engaging for a diverse audience, while the others assure that the content is of high quality and tailored to the audience.

Being Readable

To ensure that it is readable, *Taking Ownership of Your Career* avoids unnecessary jargon and research summaries. The use of straightforward language that involves the reader and a logical sequencing of the material contribute to making the material clear and understandable to you, the reader.

Being Interesting

Taking Ownership of Your Career tries to make learning easier and more enjoyable by making the material realistic and more interesting.

Being Up-to-Date

To be on the cutting edge means to have the most up-to-date material available. *Taking Ownership of Your Career* is current and timely in its content and the anecdote examples are all from current websites.

Being Accurate

Taking Ownership of Your Career is firmly grounded in research but not burdened with unnecessary references, although numerous sources are provided at the end. Careful use of research assures that the material is accurate.

Being Unique

Unlike other self-help management books, *Taking Ownership of Your Career* is intended to serve a large audience—both employees in organizations and those seeking their first jobs.

Audience

Taking Ownership of Your Career was written primarily for those looking for their first or new jobs. It is written at a level that is appropriate for individuals in either self-study, training, or classroom settings. The reader needs no special business, organizational, or technical background to understand the themes of this book. The more experience in organizations that the reader has, however, the more the reader will recognize the value of the material, but the less experience that the reader has, the more he or she probably needs the information presented in the book.

Disclaimer

This book is based on the author's research and opinions and is meant as a source of valuable information for the reader; however, it is not meant as a substitute for direct legal assistance. If such assistance is required, the services of a competent professional should be sought.

The anecdotes and cases, unless otherwise noted, are based on surveys and correspondence by the author and his earlier works: Van Fleet, D. D. 2025. *The Manager's Guide to Psychological Safety*. Business Expert Press; Van Fleet, D. D. 2024. *Dysfunctional Organizations*. Business Expert Press; Van Fleet, D. D., and E. W. Van Fleet. 2022. *Bullying and Harassment at Work: An Innovative Approach to Understanding and Prevention*. Edward Elgar Publishing; Van Fleet, E. W., and D. D. Van Fleet. 2014. *Violence at Work: What Everyone Should Know*. Information Age Publishing.

CHAPTER 1

Finding a Job

Make some notes of what you expect in this chapter. Write down what you feel is necessary to find a safe job. Keep that in mind as you read this chapter.

Before focusing on finding a safe job, you would do well to learn more about careers in general and the many jobs that are available within those careers. No single career works for everyone. Some people engage in only a single career during their lives, while others may switch between careers one or more times. While most people always work for others, some people operate their own businesses, and others do some of each. You have to discover which alternative best suits you.

Careers

Don't confuse having a career with having a life.

—Hillary Clinton

If you tend to think more about a job than a career, you are not unusual. Yet you do have a career. The term career simply refers to the attitudes and behaviors related to work experience during your life.[1] The term career can be applied to every walk of life; everyone can have a career. A secretary considering how to improve his or her current position and what that might lead to in a few years has a career in mind. A cook learning new recipes and trying to improve performance has a career. Whenever you are thinking about your current job and a future job and how to get from one to the other, you are thinking about a career. And think you should because only by thinking about your career will you be able to manage its various stages and accomplish what you want.

As the adage goes, "give me a fish, and I will eat for today; teach me to fish, and I will eat for the rest of my life."[2] Having a career goal is like learning to fish: it helps you make decisions that shape your life. Having a career goal enables you to respond to changing conditions at work. It enables you to tolerate some of the boring, frustrating, and even unsafe parts of your job because you view those as necessary steps in moving from one stage of your career to the next. It can also help you to see that your current job is not contributing to your career so that you can better plan when and how to change jobs.

Career Choice

Your initial choice of a career is important, but careers can and do change. No choice is forever. The career you decide to prepare for and follow when you are 16 may very well be different from the one you select when you are 26. That one, in turn, may be different from the one that you choose at 36 or 46, 56, 66, or even 76. But each time you change careers, there are certain factors that you will want to consider. Job security is one factor. For example, you would probably not want to start a career in a dying industry such as the manufacture of manual typewriters or horse carriages. Another factor is job safety. Few people want to work in the Army artillery because of the obvious dangers involved in it.

One aspect of career choice is which sector of the economy in which to work. Every sector of our economy needs qualified people. Employment in agriculture has fallen, but in other sectors, it has grown or fluctuated. The service sector, wholesale and retail trade, and state and local government have seen substantial increases in employment during the past 40 years. Employment in mining and the federal government has stayed relatively stable over that same period. You can also choose the military for part or all of your career. Military employment is substantial even in times of peace. Not-for-profit organizations, that have goals other than making a profit, need people, too. Religious, social service, and charitable organizations and foundations need people. You need to consider all sectors of the economy and all of these different organizations when you are making your career choice.

The degree of risk for any job, of course, varies across sectors, time, and location. In times of war, military jobs obviously are far riskier than most civilian ones. However, and more importantly, the degree of risk varies within each sector. In the military, for example, infantry soldiers and helicopter piloting are generally riskier than mechanics and desk jobs. Some organizations in "safer" sectors may, in fact, be riskier than some organizations in sectors that would appear to be less safe. Thus, limiting your job search to what appears to be a "safer" sector may not actually result in your finding a safe job, depending upon the organization at which you are employed. For instance, you might decide that pursuing your career overseas is too risky and turn down an excellent opportunity. While it is true that some overseas jobs may involve greater risk than comparable domestic ones, others have no more risk than domestic ones. Likewise, many people in the United States want more than anything else to be their own boss—to own and operate a business. Yet many small businesses operate in high-risk locations, times, or activities.

Choosing a Career

Making a career choice involves three steps. The first is understanding yourself.[3] The second is understanding possible careers and jobs. Finally, you must understand the fit between you and your career. As simple as this seems, it can be difficult to do, but you should try to go through this process periodically during your life.

Ask yourself what you really want out of life. Since you are reading this book, we assume you want some measure of safety and security at work. But just exactly what are your overall goals and aspirations? Do you want to lead a calm, peaceful life? Do you want to invent something? Do you want to be rich? What would it take to achieve what you want? Do you have the necessary skills and abilities? You need to ask yourself what you find interesting and exciting—what do you like to do? Finally, you need to ask yourself just how much or little risk you would prefer to accept in a job.

Now you need to ask these same questions about many possible careers. What do the careers you choose require in terms of skills and abilities? What do they provide people in terms of emotional involvement and excitement? What are the goals associated with various careers? A career as a professional forester may lead to very different accomplishments than a career as a politician. And, of course, some careers involve greater risks to your health and safety than others.

Finally, look for the fit between you and your career. Look for a match between your goals and those of different careers, as well as for matches in terms of interests. If you find one or more careers that match your goals and interests fairly well, examine the required skills and abilities. If you do not have those skills and abilities, can you get them by going to school or by reading? Counselors and books are available to help you work through these steps (see Recommended Readings and Bibliography).

Life Stages and Career Stages

Our lives take place in a series of stages—childhood, adolescence, young adulthood, adulthood, and senescence or old age. Each of these stages is associated with an age range, although the years are only approximate. For instance, childhood lasts until about age 13, adolescence until around age 25, and old age until we die. Movement from one stage to another can be turbulent, but things generally settle down again after each transition. Obviously, your wants and needs are likely to differ considerably from one stage to another.

Closely related to life stages are career stages. Career stages are even less exact than life stages in terms of the age at which they occur, and, of course, there is no career stage that corresponds to childhood. There are four career stages: exploration, establishment, maintenance, and decline.

Exploration is an early stage during which you develop a better understanding of yourself and various occupations. People at this stage are eager to succeed, ready to upgrade their skills through training of some kind, and generally young although they won't be if a second-career cycle is ready to occur. This stage continues through your first or entry-level job in this career cycle, which could include beginning your own business.

Establishment begins with a trial period—a continuation of the exploration stage. During this period, you might hold several jobs as you learn more about the occupational choices available. After the trial period, accomplishment and advancement occur. Now you begin to settle down in a career, learning it, and performing well. You become less dependent on others and more independent. You start to form an occupational identity and establish relationships with others in the organization.

Job hopping becomes common throughout this stage, and you may find that you can move up faster and earn more money by changing jobs. A former top executive at Walmart, Jack Shewmaker, held eight jobs in 11 years before joining Walmart. Afterward, he stayed with Walmart, and rose from district manager in 1970, when he joined the firm, to president, a position he held from 1978 until 1984.[4] Job hopping also is partly a function of companies going outside for top leaders. For example, Gould, Inc. recruited James F. McDonald from IBM to be its new CEO. In 1984, Digital Equipment Corporation brought in its new finance vice president from Ford Motor Company. A major consulting firm, the Hay Group Inc., found that companies using outsiders in key jobs exceeded rate-of-return goals more often than those that relied on insiders.[5]

Maintenance can follow one or more patterns—continued growth, leveling off, stagnation, or early decline. Career changes may result from the latter patterns, and you will start over again. People at this stage of their careers frequently begin to act as mentors for younger members of the organization, showing them the ropes and helping them along. They usually begin to reexamine their goals in life and rethink their long-term career plans.

Decline is the final stage and usually means the end of full-time employment, you face retirement and other end-of-career options. The overriding question is, "What do I do now?" You may begin a new career, or you may level off in your current career. Individuals at this stage generally begin to recognize that they are growing old and adjust in a variety of ways—some positive, such as helping others, and some not-so-positive, such as becoming indifferent or even giving up.

Career Development

Your career is important to you, and the careers of members of organizations are important to the success of those organizations. Career development is the careful, systematic approach to ensuring that sound career choices are made. It involves an individual element, career planning, and an organizational element, career management.

Career planning is much like career choice, but it is more detailed and involves carefully specifying how to move within a career once the choice has been made. How do you go about achieving success in your career? What is the route to follow? Does the area in which you begin matter? Are there certain positions in which you must be sure to gain experience? Some companies provide formal assistance in career planning.

The first thing you should do is develop a written plan. Think in terms of where you want to be at the end of some long time period—say, 20 years. Now, in order to be at that point in 20 years, where do you need to be in 10 years? Work backward to develop an answer; then work backward again to see where you need to be in five years and in one year. Knowing where you need to be in one year to achieve your 20-year goal should be vital information for shaping your decision today.

As you plan your career, you may become aware of deficiencies in your skills, experience, or abilities. You may discover, for instance, that in order to accomplish your 10-year objectives, you need to acquire a foreign language. You can start learning now. Recognizing what your deficiencies are provides you with the opportunity to rectify them through training or by moving to a new job to gain additional experience.

You should review your career plan from time to time-perhaps every three or four years, but no less frequently than every five years. This will enable you to see whether you are accomplishing your objectives; whether you need to work harder; whether you need more training, development, and experience; or whether you need to rethink your objectives. This periodic review also serves to keep your long-term objectives in your mind so that they are not driven out by short-term crises.

If you are pursuing your career within an organization, you must develop your plan in conjunction with others in the organization. Talk with those with whom you work to get their advice. If your company has a formal career management system, check with those who administer it to see whether your plan makes sense within the organization.

Career management refers to career help provided by many organizations, including business firms like Aflac, Alcoa, AT&T, Bank of America, General Electric, General Foods, General Motors, Sandvik, and Sears.[6] Career management is distinct from training and development programs, which most companies provide either in-house (that is, they do the training themselves) or by sending employees to programs conducted by trade groups, universities, or consulting firms. Career management includes career counseling, career pathing, career resources planning, and career information systems.

Career counseling can be informal or formal. Informal advice provided by a superior to a subordinate is one form; another is provided in interviews and performance evaluation sessions. A more formal method is to have special career counseling provided by a personnel department that is available to all personnel or only to those who are being moved down, up, or out of the organization.

Career pathing refers to the identification of coherent progressions of jobs-tracks, routes, or career paths that are of particular interest to the organization. As with counseling, these may be either formal or informal. The organization may specify a path that follows a particular sequence; an example is a university that states that the positions of assistant professor and associate professor are the normal progression toward becoming a full professor. Or the path may be informal, in which case "everyone knows" that you must first hold jobs A and B to get to job C.

Although they are useful for planning purposes, career paths should not be taken as absolutes. The organization that changes "normally" to "must" is unable to recognize unique situations and exceptional talent when they occur. In the past, most executives got to the top by working in only a single firm, whereas today many executives have been with several companies on their way to the top. The increasing number of women in executive positions is also bringing changes in traditional career paths. A system that is not flexible enough to permit this will prevent some extremely talented people from reaching the top.

Career resources planning refers to the use of careful planning techniques in managing the careers of others. The organization makes plans and forecasts of personnel needs, develops charts that show the planned progressions of employees, prepares inventories of human resource needs based on assessments of existing personnel, and monitors the implementation of these plans.

Career information systems are more than just internal job markets (which means that openings within the organization are announced on bulletin boards or in newsletters and memoranda, and members of the organization have a first shot at getting these jobs). Career information systems combine internal job markets with formal career counseling and the maintenance of a career information center for employees. Thus, a career information system can motivate as well as develop the organization's employees.

Companies that have formal career development programs are generally more effective in utilizing their human resources than those that do not have such programs. Additionally, these programs enable organizations to cope with the numerous government regulations concerning human resources and to recognize and respond to a wide variety of career issues.

Special Career Issues

Women and minorities have all too frequently felt that some careers were closed to them, most often because people from those groups had not yet entered those careers in sufficient numbers to set an example for others. When the potential pool of talent is artificially or arbitrarily reduced in some way, the economy suffers because organizational effectiveness is not what it might be. Therefore, it is important to recognize that members of any group can and do succeed in all careers.

More and more women work every year. Over half of the females over 16 years old are now employed, and almost half of the working population now consists of women. Both of these statistics represent huge increases from conditions at the start of this century. For that matter, there has been significant growth in recent years. Many of these women own their own businesses. In fact, women-owned businesses were one of the fastest-growing parts of the American economic scene during the 1970s and 1980s. Despite the rapid growth and the fact that nearly three million businesses are owned by women, however, while few specifics are known about the career patterns of successful businesswomen some evidence is emerging.[7] They certainly are not confined to small businesses; some women have excelled even in some of the largest corporations in the United States.[8]

Executive search firms have suggested that there are career differences between male and female corporate officers.[9] The men tend to be older and have been with their companies longer. One study found that both groups worked 55-hour weeks, although the men earned substantially more than the women. Further, most of the women felt that they had made great personal sacrifices to get where they were. Twenty percent had never married, as opposed to less than 1 percent of the men; 20 percent were separated or divorced, as opposed to about 4 percent of the men; 95 percent of the men had children, but more than half of the women were childless. Nevertheless, the number of women officers has dramatically risen over the past decade or so, and women have joined the boards of companies such as Black & Decker and SmithKline Beckman Corporation.[10] These women are experienced managers and do not hold these positions because they own or control the firms. Because there are different issues in the careers of men and women, women need to be particularly attentive to planning their careers.[11]

A recent study found more positive information regarding women in business. "Women-owned businesses continue to fuel the economy, representing 39.1 percent of all businesses—over 14 million—employing 12.2 million workers, and generating $2.7 trillion in revenue."[12] The study found that women-owned businesses are concentrated in four service industries: (1) hair and nail salons, pet care, laundries, and dry cleaners; (2) legal, bookkeeping, and consulting businesses; (3) office administration, staffing agencies, and security and surveillance services; and (4) child daycare and homecare providers, mental health practitioners, and physicians.

Members of minority groups also succeed in a wide variety of careers. Government assistance exists in a variety of forms to help members of minority groups who are interested in starting and running their own businesses. The Minority Business Development Agency was begun in the Department of Commerce in 1969. The U.S. Department of the Interior, through the Bureau of Indian Affairs, began the Indian Business Development Fund in 1970 to help American Indians secure funds for starting businesses. The Economic Development Administration began a Minority Contractors Assistance Program in 1971 to help minorities in the construction industry. Professional and technical assistance, such as accounting and engineering help, is provided under Section 406 of the Equal Opportunity Act. Some private groups, like the Cuban American Foundation and the Minority Business Development Agency (mbda.gov), are also available to assist minorities in owning their own businesses.[13]

In sum, women and minorities can and do have successful careers. Perhaps they do have particular troubles, but difficulties exist for men and Whites as well. In recent years it has been suggested that the most important action is to be seen, to be visible, noticed, and appreciated by others in your organization.

Dual incomes and dual careers also present special problems. More than half of all adult females now work. Since many of these women are married, this means that large numbers of households now have two sources of income. The economic advantages of this are obvious. Indeed, in the absence of children, there are few, if any, financial disadvantages. Problems do occur when there are children, but many companies are taking steps to alleviate some of them by providing flexible hours, more generous personal leaves, daycare centers, and the like.

Perhaps most of the problems of dual-*income* families can be worked out. If a problem arises, like a child being stricken with a long-term illness, one partner can drop out of the workforce and stay at home to nurse the child back to health. If both partners are pursuing careers, however, as opposed to merely earning income, the situation changes radically. Interrupting a career is far more devastating than interrupting a series of jobs. Which career should suffer? Whose career is less important? The adjustment for the dual-career family is not easy or obvious, and sometimes one or both partners must make a serious sacrifice of long-term goals. Even such things as scheduling vacations can become a severe problem because both parties must be able to get off at the same time.[14]

The long-term illness of a child is not a problem faced by most dual-career couples, of course. Promotions and reassignments that involve transfers to new locations are far more common and can be extremely disruptive. One partner's career may best be served by taking the new assignment, but the other partner's career may best be served by remaining. Which career is more important? What if both people are employed by the same organization, and one is a far better performer? That one is moving up rapidly, while the other moves slowly or not at all (or, even worse, gets fired). This kind of friction can tear a marriage apart.

Resolving these conflicts is not easy. It is particularly difficult now because not many people are experienced enough to offer advice, although advice is available.[15] Obviously, a key element in dual-career families is to adopt a "family" or "we/us" view rather than an "I/me" view. This might mean deciding to relocate to help partner A now with the understanding that the next major career decision will help partner B. (Of course, when partner B's turn comes, partner A may get cold feet.)

Job Hunting

With all of this in mind, then, you are ready to begin your quest for a safe job. Job hunting can be a long-drawn-out task so it's best to approach it with the idea that you will eventually be successful, but you should not be discouraged if it takes longer than you initially anticipate. You need to understand yourself—your strengths and weaknesses—in order to prepare an effective resume and cover letters as well as to be impactful during interviews. And, of course, you need to obtain information about industries and organizations to target your search for a safe job. The rest of this chapter sketches ideas to assist you with the former, while the latter topics are the primary focus of the rest of this book.

Self-Assessment

The key to useful self-assessment is honesty. Yet, despite our most honest efforts, we may not see ourselves as others see us. For this reason, it is useful to obtain the views of others, particularly others in the work environment, about our strengths and weaknesses. Try to combine both your views and those of others as you conduct your self-assessment.

What skills do you have that would appeal to a potential employer? How current are those skills? In addition to skills, what knowledge do you have that would enable you to add value to an organization? How current is that knowledge? Make a list of these and highlight keywords among those lists. Be sure that you consider knowledge and skills in technical, conceptual, interpersonal, decision making, problem solving, and all areas relevant to organizations.

Consider your priorities. You are seeking a safe job, but what would you give up to obtain such a job? Are you willing to relocate? Is your family ready to move? Will you take a reduction in compensation? If so, how much? As you consider your priorities, think about issues such as your time, the job location; travel involved; potential for new challenges; potential for advancement; who your coworkers will be; to whom you will report; what the fringe benefits are including vacation, retirement, insurance, and the like; and how secure or stable this new job might be.

Consider your career goals. In terms of your career, where do you want to be in 10 years? Five years? One year? Will this new job help you achieve those goals? Will it help you acquire the knowledge and skills you need to achieve those goals? Will it open new opportunities and/or contacts for you that will assist you in achieving your goals?

Finally, consider the types of jobs and organizations with which you are most comfortable and those with which you are least comfortable. Do you prefer small organizations or larger ones? Do you prefer highly predictable hours and working conditions or a degree of uncertainty and flexibility? Do you prefer working with people, computers, equipment, "things," or "paper?" You can no doubt identify other job and/or organizational elements that you either prefer to have or prefer to avoid in a new situation. Make a list of those and keep it ready to refer to as opportunities arise.

Preparing Your Resume and Applying for a Job

A resume is a summary of your qualifications and experience for a job. There is no one correct way to prepare a resume. Its very name clearly suggests that it is not a detailed accounting of everything that describes you and your credentials; it is a summary. Yet there is not a fixed length for one, e.g., one or two pages. You strive for completeness and brevity in the same document, and the resulting length may be from one to perhaps four or even five pages long. Old "rules" about only one page (or two) no longer apply in most fields (but you should be aware of what is the norm in your field and stick to that norm).

In the job market of today, you need two versions of your resume. A nice, clean paper version to deliver to potential employers when asked, and an electronic version to use for seeking a job online through the Internet. An electronic version of a resume is known as an e-resume and can be very useful for many job searches. You should recognize, of course, that many successful job searches have been and will continue to be conducted without the use of electronic searches and the Internet.

These two versions differ not only in the media used but also in the nature of the content. A paper resume emphasizes verbs—action words—to call the reader's attention to what you have done. An e-resume emphasizes nouns—name words—to enable people to find you easier with computerized search programs or engines. Your paper resume might say that you taught workshops or that you came up with a new advertising slogan for your current job, while your e-resume would say that you were a workshop instructor or that you are currently a copywriter in an advertising department. You should also be careful to avoid keywords (verbs or nouns) that provide information about political or religious affiliations or that suggest your views on controversial issues. You should also not include personal information about your appearance, marital status, or the like.

As you do your resume, you will find that there are actually five versions of resumes in use today—two paper versions and three electronic ones. The traditional paper resume is formatted so that it is pleasant to look at—not cramped with text from top to bottom and side to side nor with huge margins and lots of white space. Increasingly, though, organizations are asking for paper resumes that can be readily scanned into an electronic database. Scannable resumes generally use Times New Roman fonts and have no boldfacing, underlining, italics, or fancy fonts. They should also not have columns or bullets since some scanners do not handle those formatting devices very well.

An e-resume is much like a scannable paper resume. It should have little font variation and no graphics. Indeed, e-resumes are best done in plain text or ASCII (pronounced ask-ee). A formatted e-resume is also much like a formatted paper resume. It contains fonts and graphics that indicate something about your personality. Finally, some e-resumes are done as web pages. These typically are even fancier, but you should be aware that some organizations won't look at web pages. You should also be aware that some sites for uploading or posting your resume online have specific instructions that you must follow. If you don't redo your resume to fit their specifications, they will simply trash it and you will lose any opportunities that posting there would have provided. Follow any and all instructions provided by an organization, don't assume that the organization will permit you to use whatever format or approach that you are most comfortable with.

The language you use in your resume needs to be current. That tells prospective employers that you have kept your skills and knowledge up-to-date. Carefully consider what terms or phrases would catch a prospective employer's eye. These should be keywords that you should use on your resume. Be sure to use those keywords in context, however, not merely in some sort of list. Also, be careful to avoid the repetitive use of keywords; they lose their impact if they are repeated over and over. Again, remember that keywords on paper resumes are verbs while those on e-resumes are nouns.

In terms of format, you should identify and follow the current practice in your field. E-resumes should have line lengths of no more than 65 characters (remember that spaces are characters). Easy fonts to scan, fax, and so on are Times New Roman and Courier. A type size of 10 or 12 points is also best (remember that a scannable paper resume and a plain-text e-resume will have only one font and type size in the whole resume).

Current practice in your field is particularly important for determining whether or not to have a career objective and/or an introductory paragraph. Some fields use one or the other, some use neither. Always put your most recent information first (reverse chronological order—your current job, then the one before that, etc.). An e-resume may well be longer than a paper one because most will require a separate line for each piece of new information, whereas in some cases, it would be easy to put several items on the same line on a paper resume.

The order of information may vary across fields, too. A common arrangement, however, is—name, address, career objective or introductory paragraph (if common in your field), your work experience (most recent first), education (majors, minors, concentrations, and institutions), hobbies and/or interests (this is optional and a lot of people don't use it; we recommend that you not include it unless it is very common in your field), references (you should at least indicate that you can and will furnish them if asked, and, of course, obtain permission before using anyone as a reference).

Now, proofread, proofread, proofread! Resumes that have spelling errors, typographical errors, or grammar errors won't get you very far. If you prepare your resume on a computer, use its spell-checking program, but do not substitute that for actually proofreading your resume. Before submitting your resume, it is also a good idea to show it to friends or colleagues to get their reactions. They may notice something that you have overlooked.

Once you have your resume completed, you are ready to apply for jobs. In some cases, mailing or faxing your resume along with a cover letter will constitute your application [if mailing, be sure that the paper for your resume, cover letter, and envelope match]. In other cases, the organization will require you to complete an application blank. Indeed, some organizations will actually not accept your resume, they require you to use only their application blank. Upon receiving your application, most organizations will send you an Equal Employment Opportunity/Affirmative Action (EEO/AA) form to complete and send in. That information is not used in the hiring process, so you need not have any concerns about filling it out. At this stage, some organizations may telephone you to ask specific questions beyond those on application blanks.

If all goes well, you will finally be asked to come in for an interview. That, too, is an important step, so our next section provides some guidance on interviewing.

Interviewing

Always remember that the interview process is a two-way process.[16] The organization is getting the information it wants and giving you the information that it wants you to have. You should give the information sought by the organization, but you should ask questions to obtain information that you want beyond that which is furnished by the organization.

Before the interview, do your homework. Find out as much as you can about the organization, the industry in which it operates, and the specific job in which you are interested. Review your resume and your qualifications for the job and prepare answers to broad questions about yourself, e.g., "What kind of work interests you most?" "How do you plan your day?" You can find potential questions in a variety of sources.[17] Rehearse potential responses, and you may even find it helpful to practice interviewing with a friend or relative.

You should be aware that there are several different types of interviews, and you should be prepared for each of them. First, there are structured or directed interviews and unstructured or nondirected ones. The former ones follow a carefully constructed set of questions, and the interviewer will not deviate from that set. The latter are more informal and allow for more freedom of expression. Group or board interviews (two or more interviewers at once) are likely to be used when you will work in a collaborative environment (the former at lower organizational levels than the latter). Stress interviews may be used if the position is going to be one in which significant stress is likely to be encountered and the organization is attempting to determine how well you handle stress. Typically, such interviews involve rapid-fire questions with little time to consider answers and tricky questions designed to be "turned back" on you. Some employers like to use stress interviews for all positions, and you should carefully consider whether or not you would be comfortable working for such employers. There are also telephone interviews. These may be any one of those above, with the difference being that they are conducted by telephone instead of in person. Essentially, all of the recommendations presented here (with the exception of how to dress) are as applicable to a telephone interview as one conducted face-to-face.

The day of the interview be sure to leave early to make certain that unforeseen events don't cause you to be late. It is far better to be early than late. Be well groomed and dress appropriately for the type of organization and job. Don't snack while waiting and don't chew gum or smoke. If you use a breath mint, dispose of it before the interview starts. Make sure that you have copies of your resume and your list of references in case more than one person is involved in the interview process.

Shake hands as you meet the interviewer(s), and make sure you remember his or her name. During the interview, respond promptly, but if a question requires some thought before answering, by all means, take your time to think. Speak clearly and listen carefully. Be truthful, but don't put yourself down. Show enthusiasm for the organization and the job, as well as a willingness to be cooperative. Have your questions in mind—you may even have them on note cards to consult during the interview—and ask them when it seems appropriate. As the interview concludes, thank the interviewer.

After the interview, make careful notes of everything that was said. Points may emerge that are not clear, and you need to be prepared to obtain clarification when (if?) your next contact occurs. Send a short letter of thanks within a day or so of the interview and follow up with a tele-phone call a week or so after that. Finally, evaluate yourself so that you can do even better in your next interview.

Good Luck!

From here, I wish you luck. Frequently, that's what it takes at this stage because there are so many qualified people seeking the same jobs. Be sure to follow up with prospective employers, just in case.

Chapter Takeaways

- Your choice of a career is important, but careers can and do change.
- Understand yourself.
- Understand possible careers and jobs.
- Understand the fit between you and your career.
- There are four career stages: exploration, establishment, mainte-nance, and decline.
- Do a self-assessment.
- Prepare for interviews.

Think About This Chapter Again

Look over the notes you took before reading this chapter. What changes would you make now?

Think about the following anecdotes in relation to this chapter.

"Trying to stay positive with so many rejections can and will put you into depression, it's tough to go out every single day and look for work. Go to a temp service, to make a few bucks … and tell yourself all those rejections were meant to be, it's not your calling to work there. Your well-being suffers the most, and that's the most important part to make sure you are all right.

The go-getter really does win more, so do little steps, go door to door, 2 hours a day, call 2 hours a day, surf the net 2 hours … and that's enough. do it every day. focus, make a feasible plan, follow up on your callbacks, and keep records of all you do. In the next 6 hours, earn your keep, maybe cut grass, shovel snow, run errands, and babysit. If you earn a little you will feel so much better, it's a struggle you will face.

Treat it like a business, don't take it personally if you don't find work, and do not lay blame. The right job will come along, hard work and sheer determination wins in the end."

Source: Adopted from https://www.quora.com/What-is-your-experience-in-job-hunting.

"Last year, I broke a cardinal rule: never quit a job without another lined up. Leaving a stable position wasn't easy, but travelling and studying in New York over the summer was an opportunity I couldn't turn down. Your twenties are for taking risks and I fully embraced that.

That was until my adventure ended and I felt the immense weight of uncertainty—a tough reality for a type-A personality with back-up plans for back-up plans. After tweaking countless cover letters, I spiralled into self-doubt. Meticulously tracking applications like packages I desperately needed wasn't helping my sanity but with all the time in the world, what else could I do?

In hindsight, I fell into the trap of equating job rejections with personal failure, as repeated knockbacks chipped away at my self-worth. I can't emphasize enough, that much like dating, job rejection isn't a measure of your worth. It's vital to resist the narrative that hard work guarantees success, as this belief falsely ties self-worth to career achievements.

Struggling to find work is not a personal or moral failing and hiring isn't strictly merit-based; even strong candidates face rejection due to factors beyond their control, like budget constraints or another applicant's niche skills. While optimising your resume matters, nothing is more important than prioritising your mental health and resilience. Visualise success and pursue side quests to nurture your self-development.

After a few months of side quests, I'm happy to report that I've landed a Cadetship at the ABC, beginning in February. And I'm even happier to confirm that all those people who said, 'It's the economy, not you,' were absolutely right."

Source: Adopted from https://fashionjournal.com.au/life/positive-job-hunt/.

Recommended Reading

The following could expand your understanding of the chapter's material:

Bolles, R. N. 1980. *What Color Is Your Parachute?* Ten Speed Press.

Burnett, B., and D. Evans. 2016. *Designing Your Life: How to Build a Well-Lived, Joyful Life.* Alfred A. Knopf.

Cannings, K., and C. Montmarquette. 1991. "Managerial Momentum: A Simultaneous Model of the Career Progress of Male and Female Managers." *Industrial and Labor Relations Review*, January 1, 212–228.

Cole, D. 1990. "Assess Your Skills to Reduce Career Doubts." *The Wall Street Journal, The College Edition of the National Business Employment Weekly*, Spring, 7–8.

CHAPTER 2

Health and Safety at Work—Should You Be Concerned? Is It a Problem?

Make some notes of what you expect in this chapter. Write down what you feel is necessary to determine what comprises a safe job. Keep that in mind as you read this chapter.

Looking for a job at any time is a daunting task, but it is especially so during economic and social difficult times. One site (see below) identifies the best and worst jobs that you could use as a place to get started. When pandemic or recession conditions are taken into account, the outlook can be quite different. However, because different methods were employed, some jobs appear as both "worst" and "financially secure" (teacher, corporate employee, and nurse).

Best and Worst Jobs of 2023

(www.myperfectresume.com/career-center/careers/basics/worst-jobs)

1. Software developer—annual mean wage: $120,990
2. Lawyer—annual mean wage: $148,030
3. Teacher—annual mean wage: $36,460 to $133,310
4. Administrative assistant—annual mean wage: $41,080 to $66,870
5. Nurse—annual mean wage: $123,780
6. Police officer
7. Operations manager
8. Medical assistant
9. Bookkeeper

10. Marketing specialist

11. Cashier

12. Electrician

13. Mechanic

14. Stocking associate

15. Office clerk

16. Store associate

17. Carpenter

18. Bartender

19. Customer service representative

20. Construction worker

21. Truck driver—annual mean wage: $42,630 to $50,340

22. Laborer—annual mean wage: $31,440 to $44,130

23. Janitor—annual mean wage: $31,860

24. Waiter/waitress—annual mean wage: $29,010

25. Cleaner—annual mean wage: $29,580 to $38,530

Challenging times like pandemics and recessions impact some jobs or occupations negatively while others seem to flourish. Terrell[1] identifies occupations that are negatively impacted by the recent pandemic (Table 2.1), while Rugaber[2] notes those likely to expand during those same difficult periods (Table 2.2). Here, too, some jobs or occupations appear both as harmed and helped (sales workers, retail workers; health care workers, personal care aides, physical therapy assistants, and registered nurses). In addition, there are likely to be differential location impacts so that a job may be unavailable in one area but in demand in another. So, you need to be as flexible as possible, both in terms of the types of jobs you may be seeking and the locations at which those jobs may be available.

Looking to the future, jobs that should be available include integrated health and wellness administrator, chief sustainability officer, director of remote work, and remote culture keeper.[3] Others might be chief HR technology optimization officer, experience engineering specialist, data science manager, chatbot coach, chief purpose officer, algorithm bias finder, educational resilience leader, robot manager, home office consultant, and home and family security consultant.[4]

Table 2.1 Occupations impacted negatively by pandemic

Service workers
Arts, design, entertainment, and media workers
Small business owners
Construction or mining workers
Sales workers
Transportation workers
Manufacturing or production workers
Installation, maintenance, or repair workers
Health care workers
Clerical or office workers

Source: Terrell (2020)

Table 2.2 Jobs that grow during pandemic and recession

Factory floor technicians
Temporary help agencies
Professional and technical services
Network engineers
Information technology professionals

When you leave college, there are thousands of people out there with the same degree you have; when you get a job, there will be thousands of people doing what you want to do for a living. But you are the only person alive who has sole custody of your life.

—*Anna Quindlen*

A Safe Job

Regardless of where your job search may lead, you almost certainly want to feel safe while on the job. Why would you have an interest in a safe job? More broadly, why should anyone be concerned about safe jobs? There was a time when citizens could feel safe at work unless, perhaps, they were employed in a high-risk job like law enforcement, the fire service, the military, or construction. Indeed, many organizations have developed policies dealing with safety.

Policies

The following are two examples of what an organization's safety and health policy might look like. However, your organization or one that you are interested in might have one that is different.

Organization A

1. The Organization's policy is to ensure a safe, healthful workplace for all employees. The organization employs effective accident and illness prevention programs that involve everyone to eliminate workplace hazards.
2. The organization's management will be held accountable for the prevention of workplace incidents, injuries, and illnesses. Upper-level management will provide support for safety program initiatives and will consider all employee suggestions for achieving a safer, healthier workplace. Managers will keep informed about workplace safety and health hazards and will regularly review the organization's safety and health program.
3. Supervisors are responsible for training workers in safe work practices and seeing that those practices are carried out. Supervisors enforce safety rules and work to eliminate hazardous conditions.
4. The organization has a safety committee that includes employer and employee representatives who recommend improvements for safety and health in the workplace. The committee also identifies hazards and unsafe work practices, removes obstacles to incident prevention, and helps the organization evaluate the safety and health program.

5. All members of the organization are expected and encouraged to participate in safety and health program activities, including reporting hazards, unsafe work practices, and accidents immediately to supervisors or the safety committee; wearing required personal protective equipment, and participating in and supporting safety committee activities.

Organization B

The safety and health of our employees is this company's most important business consideration. No employee will be required to do a job that they consider unsafe. The company will comply with all the applicable Oregon OSHA workplace safety and health requirements and maintain occupational safety and health standards that equal or exceed the industry's best practices. The company will establish a safety committee, consisting of management and labor representatives, whose responsibility will be to identify hazards and unsafe work practices, remove obstacles to accident prevention, and evaluate the company's effort to achieve an accident-and-injury-free workplace.

The company pledges to do the following:

- Strive to achieve the goal of zero accidents and injuries.
- Provide mechanical and physical safeguards wherever they are necessary.
- Conduct routine safety and health inspections to find and eliminate unsafe working conditions, control health hazards, and comply with all applicable OR-OSHA safety and health requirements.
- Train all employees in safe work practices and procedures.
- Provide employees with necessary personal protective equipment and train them to use and care for it properly.
- Enforce company safety and health rules and require employees to follow the rules as a condition of employment.
- Investigate accidents to determine the cause and prevent similar accidents.

Managers, supervisors, and all other employees share responsibility for a safe and healthy workplace.

- Management is accountable for preventing workplace injuries and illnesses. Management will consider all employee suggestions for achieving a safer, healthier workplace. Management will also keep informed about workplace safety-and-health hazards and regularly review its safety and health program.
- Supervisors are responsible for supervising and training workers in safe work practices.
- Supervisors must enforce company rules and ensure that employees follow safe practices during their work.
- Employees are expected to participate in safety and health program activities including, immediately reporting hazards, unsafe work practices, and accidents to supervisors or a safety committee representative, wearing required personal protective equipment, and, participating in and supporting safety committee activities.

There was a time when mothers and fathers taught their children that they would be safe if they went to work or school and "stayed out of trouble." Today, you may have a responsible, high-paying, accident-free job in a high-class company located in a high-rent district and still be unsafe. The only machine you operate may be a computer, and you could still face a debilitating illness from your job. You may make a business trip to another company location or another country's office and encounter a terrorist bomb. Unfortunately, all jobs are not entirely safe, and everyone should be concerned about safe jobs. There are lots of seen and unseen aspects of jobs that could render them unsafe, including stress, accidents, violence, and terrorism.

Stress

"Job stress can be defined as the harmful physical and emotional responses that occur when the requirements of the job do not match the capabilities, resources, or needs of the worker."[5] After reorganization, downsizing, or restructuring, employees are expected to assume more duties and work longer hours with no change in their pay. Adult employees at a chicken processing plant are not permitted to take restroom breaks without raising their hands to get permission from supervisors. In some cases, such permission is not obtained in time to prevent them from soiling themselves. Mandatory overtime is required by many employers, placing a burden on employees but particularly those with families with small children.

Some companies substantially restrict employees from talking to one another while at work. In order to hold many jobs, employees are expected to work irregular hours with frequent shift changes. Employees are expected to perform routine equipment maintenance that involves working with solvents that could be absorbed through the skin and/or give off dangerous, even flammable fumes. Workers receive ambiguous job instructions and performance feedback consisting of such statements as "Do the best you can." "If you don't show significant improvement, we'll have to find someone else for that job."

There are so many different types of people from so many different groups at the workplace that it is difficult to communicate, let alone develop meaningful relationships with coworkers off the job. Making a wrong decision can get you fired, yet all too often, you have to make fast decisions with far less information than you feel is necessary to have any confidence in your decision being correct.

Accidents

One of the most common causes of an unsafe workplace is accidents. Accidents at work refer to "an unplanned incident or event that leads to the injury of an employee and/or damage to a company's property."[6] Consider some incidents about jobs and work that have been in the news.

- A worker in West Virginia is injured while operating a table saw that had no safety guard. He had complained that it was unsafe but was threatened with termination if he refused to do the work.
- Approximately 8 percent of all private-sector employees will suffer lost time during any given year due to injuries or illness.

- Two Texas workers are killed in a trench cave-in due to the company's failure to adequately support the trench walls.
- Over a million American workers each year suffer disabling injuries.
- A group of Georgia workers suffered from lead poisoning that the company's physician had known about but did nothing about and even intentionally hid the information from them.
- A punch press worker lost his right hand when the press unexpectedly came down as he was cleaning it.
- Thousands of workers have fatal accidents at work each year.
- While moving out of an office, an employee lifts a box and ruptures a spinal disk necessitating surgery and a life of continuing pain.
- Workers using desktop computers extensively find increasing incidences of tingling, numbness, and severe pain in their wrists and hands—carpal tunnel syndrome is a frequent diagnosis.

Violence

According to the Occupational Safety and Health Administration, workplace violence consists of any act or threat of physical violence, harassment, intimidation, or other threatening disruptive behavior that occurs at the work site.[7] It can range from threats and verbal abuse to physical assaults and even homicide

- Shouting "everyone is going to die," a fired Fort Lauderdale maintenance employee walked into a meeting of his former coworkers, chased them around the office, and methodically shot them—killing five and injuring another.
- An employee at Seal Master of Hawaii returned to his former workplace after being fired from his job. He shot and seriously wounded his former supervisor and held five coworkers hostage for six hours.
- In Maine, a former mental patient turned down for a job at a convent was accused of beating and stabbing four nuns, killing two of them by "multiple blunt force injuries to the head."

- A year after being fired at a bank credit card center for sexual harassment, an Ohio man forced his way into the homes of former coworkers, fatally shooting four individuals (including a 4-month-old girl) and wounding two others.
- A female teacher was left dead and a second critically wounded after an expelled student at a South Carolina high school returned to the school building and started shooting. He then turned the gun on himself and committed suicide.
- A young male accountant in California, only on the job for six weeks, shot and killed his female supervisor, then committed suicide with the same gun, one day after receiving his first performance counseling session.
- A "quiet, unassuming" 58-year-old postal worker who had been on the job for 22 years shot and killed his supervisor in California and then quietly surrendered to his coworkers.
- In Virginia, a civilian Navy employee shot his boss and a co-worker in their workplace before committing suicide with the same handgun.
- A man in Seattle shot and killed his pregnant wife and two of her friends who were waiting to testify at his annulment hearing outside a Seattle courtroom.

Terrorism

Terrorism occurring at work has usually referred to a few companies operating overseas that occasionally have to deal with political and criminal terrorists from foreign countries.[8] More recently, internal terrorism has been identified.[9] It is different from other forms of dysfunctional behavior at work in that its purpose is to evoke fear or extreme stress in order to bring about a change that reflects the perpetrator's own views. The following are some examples of terrorism at work.

- Numerous American businesspeople working abroad in the late 1970s and early 1980s were kidnapped. Some were tortured, some were freed only after sizable ransom payments were made, and at least three were murdered while in captivity.

- A Denver talk-show host was machine-gunned to death in his driveway by members of "The Order" who opposed views expressed on his program.
- American citizens were kidnapped and held hostage in Lebanon. They were chained, imprisoned in the dark, beaten, and denied medical care for years. Three of them were murdered during their captivity, although others eventually were released.
- Pan American Flight 103 was destroyed over Lockerbie, Scotland, by terrorists, killing 259 people from 30 nations; another 11 persons perished on the ground.
- In a series of attacks during the late 1990s, toxic gas was released in Japanese subways, killing ten and injuring thousands. A Japanese terrorist group indicated that it planned to use such tactics to accomplish its goals.
- In one two-year period, five people at abortion clinics were killed, 11 wounded. Buildings housing abortion clinics are frequently bombed and burned.
- In 1996 A pipe bomb exploded at the Olympics in Atlanta, Georgia, killing one person, causing another to die of a heart attack, and injuring over a hundred others.
- The president of Sanyo Video Components (USA) Corporation was abducted at its Tijuana, Mexico, plant and held for a $2 million ransom by a ring of Mexican gunmen.
- Late in 1996, a terrorist group entered the Japanese embassy in Lima, Peru, taking more than 600 hostages. Over a period of months, those hostages were released, although some were not freed until nearly half a year later.

Summary

These sorts of incidents are becoming all too common events in organizational life. As a result, many people—you included—have become interested in learning more about job safety and, in particular, which jobs seem to present the lowest risk to people holding those jobs. This book is about how to look for a safe (at least a relatively safe) and job safety on the job.

Chapter Takeaways

- Best and worst jobs.
- Safety and health policy.
- Incidents: stress, accidents, violence, terrorism.

Think About This Chapter Again

Look over the notes you took before reading this chapter. What changes would you make now?

Think about these anecdotes in relation to this chapter.

"Job hunting can feel overwhelming, especially when you're sending out lots of applications without hearing back. But one thing I've noticed is that persistence is key. Sometimes, it's about staying organized, keeping track of where you applied, and following up. It's also important to stay positive even when rejections come your way. Networking is often a game-changer too. Many people land jobs through connections, so reaching out to friends or colleagues can open doors you wouldn't have expected."

Source: Adopted from www.quora.com/What-is-your-experience-in-job-hunting

---

"I've always felt quite in control in my life, or at least when I'm not, I tend to 'trust' in the universe that all will be well. However, with my career, I could never accept that it would just 'work out.' I struggled to juggle the pull and tug between creative, academic, and corporate pathways when I left university. I wasn't sure where it was I wanted to end up. I felt like I had all of this passion, willpower, ambition, and drive with nowhere to direct it. I tried to do so many things at once as if it were a process of elimination, and in all of them, I felt detached.

I was on a major job hunt after moving states (which was the push to quit the several jobs I had at once) and I landed a management position in a retail store. It was a great place to meet people in a new city, though it very quickly motivated me to start applying again, and this time with purpose. I was applying for both creative and corporate roles, ready for anything that came my way. But soon, the job hunt became monotonous and I turned to AI to write my cover letters. I was churning them out.

Then, on Ethical Jobs, I came across a job advertisement for Humans of Purpose. It was a little ambiguous but something in me knew I had to put myself out there, be bold and go for it. I have never been more authentic or heartfelt in a cover letter and application in my life. I tried complete [sic] honestly and it worked.

If you're in a similar boat, my advice is to ride it out. Something will come along and though the wait is shit, there is an end. Know what you're looking for and stay steadfast in that. I've learned that when I'm comfortable enough, I might not make the necessary effort to get to where I want to be. By making the situation dire, a little worse, a little more uncomfortable, dare I say desperate, you'll haul ass to get to where you need to be."

Source: Adopted from https://fashionjournal.com.au/life/positive-job-hunt/

Recommended Reading

The following could expand your understanding of the chapter's material:

Duncan, M., and P. Heighway. 2014. *Health and Safety at Work Essentials.* 8th ed. Lawpack Publishing.

Fuller, T. P. 2019. *Global Occupational Safety and Health Management Handbook.* Taylor & Francis Group.

Manuele, F. A. 2003. *On the Practice of Safety.* 3rd ed. Wiley-Interscience.

CHAPTER 3

Accidents, Careers, and Jobs

Make some notes of what you expect in this chapter. Write down why you feel a lack of accidents is part of a safe job. Keep that in mind as you read this chapter.

> "[There are] … four people named Everybody, Somebody, Anybody, and Nobody. There was an important job to be done and Everybody was asked to do it. Everybody was sure Somebody would do it. Anybody could have done it, but Nobody did it. Somebody got angry about that because it was Everybody's job. Everybody thought Anybody could do it, but Nobody realized that Everybody would not do it. It ended up that Everybody blamed Somebody when Nobody did what Anybody could have done."[1]

The important job to be done is to assure the health and safety of employees in organizations. All too frequently, safety is not a high priority in organizations, and Nobody really does it. For that reason, you need to find out about accidents and jobs.

Causes

The more common causes of workplace accidents include overexertion from carrying or lifting heavy items; falls on stairs, landings, or roofs; slips and trips that result in strains, sprains, or broken bones; falling objects; and, of course, repetitive motion that can lead to carpal tunnel syndrome and chronic back or shoulder pain.[2]

Accidents could be the result of an unsafe condition, an unsafe act, or an act of God. Rarely are they caused by acts of God; the majority are caused by the unsafe acts of people.[3] Acts of God include snowstorms, rains, lightning, floods, high winds, and high tides. Unsafe conditions include such things as inadequate guards on equipment, congested worksites, inadequate warning devices, fire and explosion hazards, poor housekeeping, hazardous atmospheric conditions, excessive noise, radiation exposure, and inadequate illumination or ventilation. Unsafe acts include operating equipment without authority, failure to warn of danger or to secure a worksite from danger, operating equipment at improper speed, improper lifting, attempting to service equipment that is in motion, horseplay, drinking alcohol or drug intake, failure to wear protective equipment, using defective equipment, and removing safety guards.

Because it is well-established that the unsafe acts of people are the primary cause of accidents, engineers, psychologists, sociologists, and others have studied accidents extensively. Among the concepts that came from this work was the suggestion that some people behaved in ways to have more accidents than did others—they were accident-prone. In addition, some researchers felt that people had accidents as an unconscious way of withdrawing or avoiding work,[4] although more recent work seems to dispute that view.[5]

From both an individual and an organizational point of view, the root causes of accidents clearly have been attributed to people. Indeed, the "four horsemen of safety" reflect this view. They are Apathy, lack of concern or indifference; Complacency, content or lack of vigilance; Distraction, inattention or absent-mindedness; and Deviation, taking shortcuts or willfulness.[6] Despite the fact that both individuals and organizations can engage in activities that result in accidents, most experts agree that the final responsibility for workplace health and safety lies with management.[7] Indeed, the basis of federal regulation in the area of health and safety is voluntary compliance by the management of organizations.

Voluntary compliance, of course, means that there will be variation in the diligence with which managers seek to ensure safe working conditions. Because of technological and environmental differences, there will also be differences in accident rates across industries and jobs. You will need to consider all aspects of accident histories as you consider what might be safer jobs.

Accident Rates

One problem with dealing with accidents is information. The information may not be available. The information you do obtain may not be comparable across jobs, companies, or industries. Indeed, who reports the information, over what time period, how it is presented, and so on are of great concern in the health and safety area.

The National Safety Council, the Occupational Safety and Health Administration, and industry safety associations, however, have been working to arrive at standards that yield more comparable data. You need to be careful to consider the source of any accident and safety information that you receive. So long as you are careful with regard to sources and don't regard any source of data as absolute, you should be able to make reasonable comparisons and decisions.

With that in mind, then, let's examine some data. We will consider industries first and then more specific organizations.

Industries

One common measure of the accident rate for whole industries is the nonfatal occupational injury and illness rate reported by the U.S. Bureau of Labor Statistics. Those rates for many industries in 2023 are shown in Table 3.1 at the end of this chapter and Table 3.2 has similar data from the National Safety Council. In general, the highest rates are among the manufacturing and construction industries, while the lowest rates are among the finance and insurance industries.

Some of the greatest variation exists among service industries. Legal, insurance, engineering, and management services tend to have very low injury and illness rates. Social services and miscellaneous repair services tend to be about average. Health, amusement and recreation services, while not high, do tend to be above average.

Transportation industries also display variation. Pipelines and transportation services are low. Water transportation is near the average. Local passenger transit, air transportation, and trucking, on the other hand, are relatively high.

You should note that these are very broad industry classifications, too. That means that there is no doubt considerable variation within each of these classifications. Indeed, even within a narrower industry classification, there is likely to be variation across organizations, and within any given organization, there will be variation across jobs.

Table 3.1 Incidence Rates of nonfatal occupational injuries and illnesses by industry and cases, 2023

Industry	NAICS code	Cases
All industries including private, state, and local government		2.7
Private industry		2.4
Goods-producing		2.7
Natural resources and mining		3.0
Agriculture, forestry, fishing, and hunting	11	4.2
Mining, quarrying, and oil and gas extraction	21	1.3
Construction	23	2.3
Manufacturing	31–33	2.8
Wholesale trade	42	2.3
Retail trade	44–45	3.1
Transportation and warehousing	48–49	4.5
Utilities	22	1.8
Information	51	1.0
Finance and insurance	52	0.3
Real estate and rental and leasing	53	2.0
Professional, scientific, and technical services	54	0.8
Management of companies and enterprises	55	0.6
Administrative and support and waste management	56	1.8
Educational services	61	1.7
Health care and social assistance	62	3.6
Arts, entertainment, and recreation	71	4.3
Accommodation and food services	72	2.7
Other services (except public administration)	81	1.7
State and local government		4.3
State government		3.0
Goods-producing		4.0
Service-providing		3.0
Educational and health services		2.8
Educational and health services		4.0
Public administration	92	5.9

Source: Bureau of Labor Statistics, U.S. Department of Labor, Survey of Occupational Injuries and Illnesses in cooperation with participating state agencies.

Table 3.2 *Preventable injuries at work by industry, United States, 2023*

Industry division	Hours worked[a] (millions)	Deaths[a]		Deaths per 100,000 full-time equivalent workers[a]		Medically consulted injuries
		2023	Change from 2022	2023	Change from 2022	
All industries	298,700	4,543	−3%	3.0	−6%	4,070,000
Agriculture[b]	4,300	430	8%	20.0	10%	90,000
Mining[b]	1,300	113	0%	17.4	8%	10,000
Construction	22,400	1,029	1%	9.2	0%	260,000
Manufacturing	31,200	351	−3%	2.3	−4%	440,000
Wholesale trade	6,600	161	3%	4.9	−2%	80,000
Retail trade	28,800	183	5%	1.3	8%	450,000
Transportation and warehousing	14,400	893	−13%	11.7	−9%	320,000
Utilities	2,500	39	8%	3.1	−9%	20,000
Information	5,400	23	−43%	0.9	−44%	30,000
Financial activities	21,000	75	6%	0.7	0%	70,000
Professional and business services	38,200	555	6%	2.9	7%	210,000
Educational and health services	46,600	149	15%	0.6	0%	790,000
Leisure and hospitality	22,600	165	−13%	1.5	−17%	330,000
Other services[b]	13,300	162	7%	2.4	4%	110,000
Government	40,100	332	−6%	1.7	−6%	860,000
Industry not reported by BLS		8	−27%			

[a]Deaths include persons of all ages. Workers and death rates include persons 16 years and older. The rate is calculated as: (Number of fatal work injuries × 200,000,000/Total hours worked). The base for 100,000 full-time equivalent workers is 200,000,000 hours. Prior to 2008, rates were based on estimated employment—not hours worked.
[b]Agriculture includes forestry, fishing, and hunting. Mining includes oil and gas extraction. "Other services" excludes public administration.
Source: NSC analysis of data from the BLS CFOI surveillance program.

Take risks: if you win, you will be happy; if you lose, you will be wise.
—Author Unknown

Organizations

Endeavor Business Media identified eight companies as "safest" in 2024. They were Arcadis U.S., AtkinsRéalis US Nuclear, Brieser Construction, Burns & McDonnell, The Clorox Company, D. C. Taylor Co., United Engineers & Constructors, and Victaulic.[8]

AlertMedia noted Dalkia Energy Solutions, Texas Roadhouse, and Moss Construction as examples of companies with great safety cultures.[9] The Haws Corporation named five companies as "safest."[10] They were The AES Corporation, Alan Shintani Inc., Aqueos Corporation, BL Harbert International, and The Charles Stark Draper Laboratory Inc. The SHRM (Society for Human Resource Management) provides a website where you can compare and research workplace safety companies and businesses for 35 companies.

Costs

Accidents are costly. The direct costs of such accidents are obvious, but accidents result in indirect costs as well. Those indirect or less obvious costs may well be greater than the more obvious ones. Those indirect costs could include such things as:

- Administrative time spent on paperwork and interviews
- Damage to tools, equipment, and other property
- Economic loss to injured worker's family
- Failure to meet production targets or to complete projects
- Legal fees
- Loss of morale and efficiency due to break-up of group or team
- Lost time by those involved and any other employees
- Medical expenses
- Overhead cost (while work was disrupted)

- Spoiled work
- Time lost for replacing damaged equipment or from work by injured employee(s)
- Training costs for new workers if necessary
- Workers' compensation premiums and increases in them

Information to Seek

A safe job is certainly one for which you would expect a low level of accidents. So, if you are interested in a safe job, you should seek information about accidents and safety for any job for which you are interested. Some of the questions for which you may wish to seek answers are the following.

- Has this organization ever received an OSHA citation?
- If so, how was it handled?
- What is this organization's safety philosophy? What is its safety program?
- What is the accident record for this organization?
- How does that compare to others in the field?
- What is the accident record for this particular job?
- How does that compare to similar jobs in other organizations?
- What are the normal working conditions for this job?
- Does this job ever encounter unsafe conditions?
- What is the role of my potential supervisor in accident prevention?
- What kind of insurance and/or worker's compensation applies in case you have an accident on this job?

Chapter Takeaways

- Causes of accidents.
- Accident rates by industry and specific organizations.
- Costs of accidents.
- Sources of information.

Think About This Chapter Again

Look over the notes you took before reading this chapter. What changes would you make now?

Think about these anecdotes in relation to this chapter.

"At age 57, I applied for a contract job with a governmental agency (county government). The interview panel impressed me immediately with the diversity: there was a woman a little older than myself, and several younger employees, more than half of whom were persons of color. The management interview panel that followed was three women, two of whom were my age or older. Since being hired as a permanent employee at age 58, I have had nothing but positive experiences with my employer's diversity and equal opportunity for all. Working in high tech, most of my previous working environments have been in groups of men, usually white, and always young; I have some real horror stories about some of my prior companies! It is refreshing to work in a culture where experience is valued, and having a personal life is appreciated more than working 60-hour weeks. Some say it's impossible to find work in high-tech after age 50, but that has not been my experience. Yes, lots of companies are scornful of older workers, but that is less prevalent in the public sector. I do think my current employer is particularly good in recognizing and valuing diversity, largely because of policies that come from our county executive. I've since moved from contract to career service (permanent) status. An additional feature of public service is that we are union-represented so once someone is through the probationary period, the job is more secure than most private sector employment."

Source: Adopted from www.vocationvillage.com/anti-ageism-job-search-success -stories/

"My path to working in media is quite unusual. Until October 2023, I was a kindergarten teacher undertaking a master's in early childhood education. During my lunch breaks and work commutes, I wrote articles and edited videos for publications like *Fashion Journal, Frankie,* and *Refinery29 Australia.* In October of that year, the boss at *Refinery29 Australia* asked me to apply for their social producer role, and within a week I had the job. I was there until my 25th birthday in 2024 when I was made redundant as the publication shut down. This was also great timing for a quarter-life crisis.

I'm in a privileged position to live at home with my parents, so I had the space to wallow in the sadness and allow myself to feel the loss. I had probably ten business days of scrapbooking, watching *My Lady Jane,* and indulging in many sweet treats to make myself feel better. However, I was still productive at this time. I was responding to e-mails, pitching articles and videos to other publications, and chatting with friends who had been through the media ringer of redundancies and budget cuts.

I think by continuing to write and make videos, I was keeping my name out there and showcasing my tenacity. I think you need to allow yourself to feel every emotion but not get stuck in the trap of feeling sorry for yourself because that doesn't help in the long run (as soothing as it can be in the moment). Keep on doing what you love and if you keep backing yourself, the right job will come to you.

Within a month of my redundancy era, I was hired at *Missing Perspectives* to be a part-time social media producer and I have been a regular contributor at *Fashion Journal.* I think what's important at this time is to trust that good things are around the corner. If you had told me that by the end of the year, I would have met and interviewed at the NGV Gala, I would have pissed myself laughing. By riding the wave, I was able to find work that I love and find joy in my work again."

Source: Adopted from https://fashionjournal.com.au/life/positive-job-hunt/

Recommended Reading

The following could expand your understanding of the chapter's material:

Hagan, Phillip E., J. F. Montgomery, and J. T. O'Reilly. 2001. *Accident Prevention Manual.* National Safety Council.

Patrontasch, B. n.d. "Workplace Accident: A Comprehensive Guide." *https://www.myshyft.com/glossary/workplace-accident/.*

Serrette, S. 2001. "Planning and Organizing a Safety Program." *Occupational Health and Safety* 70 (7): 26–30.

CHAPTER 4

Stress, Careers, and Jobs

Make some notes of what you expect in this chapter. Write down what you feel is the relation of stress to safe jobs. Keep that in mind as you read this chapter.

Stress is not a simple phenomenon.[1] Stress refers to individual responses to strong stimuli. The stimuli are called stressors. While some stress can be positive—it can motivate you to work to your top level of performance—other stress or too much stress clearly is negative. Positive stress is beneficial, whereas negative stress can be harmful if it is not recognized and dealt with at an early stage. You should also understand that stress can be caused by "good" as well as "bad" things. Receiving a promotion with a raise and then having to decide what to do with the money can be stressful. Excessive pressure, unreasonable demands on your time, and bad news can all cause stress. And, of course, a pandemic with associated economic and social hardships is a major source of stress.

Positive stress is experienced by meeting deadlines, becoming more innovative, being more productive, and accepting challenges. Negative stress occurs when the pressures of life, including work, increase to a level where the individual can no longer cope. Hence pressure is healthy until it exceeds the person's ability to cope, and then it can cause illness.

Negative stress can be seriously debilitating, and the effects can be long lasting. Management and organizations suffer because of absenteeism, reduced productivity, increased compensation premiums—medical insurance based on stress are higher than other claims. Thus, our discussion here focuses on negative stress—the form you want to avoid.

Many of life's failures are people who did not realize how close they were to success when they gave up.

—*Thomas Edison*

Causes

As shown in Table 4.1 at the end of this chapter, about 100,000 chemicals; some 50 physical factors; 200 biological factors; some 20 adverse ergonomic conditions; a similar number of physical factors such as workloads, quotas, deadlines, details, competitiveness, speed required, precision, initiative, win/lose situations degree of confinement, and energy and stamina requirements; lifting; machines or tools used; hazards; putting one's own or another's life at risk; outdoor work; environmental conditions; and associated numbers and types of psychological and social factors such as working in the public eye, meeting the public, having to work with people you dislike, and degree of participation have been identified as sources of stress at work. These contribute to the risk of occupational injuries, diseases and stress reactions, job dissatisfaction, and absence of well-being.

In 2025, low-stress jobs include marketing manager, industrial engineer, IT manager, web developer, computer network architect, sales manager, community health worker, social and community service manager, mechanical engineer, accountant, mental health counselor, electrical engineer, architectural and engineering manager, librarian, and hearing aid specialist.[2] Most of the physical and environmental sources of stress can and should be prevented. Nevertheless, they exist, and you need to try to understand which are most likely to cause your personal stress and which are most likely to exist in jobs for which you are interested and qualified. So, let's examine some of these in a bit more detail by examining four overlapping categories—task, physical, role, and interpersonal stressors.

Tasks

Some jobs and occupations are inherently more stressful than others. Having to make fast decisions, decisions with less than complete information, or decisions that have relatively serious consequences are some of the things that can make some jobs stressful. Having a heavy physical workload or unergonomic working conditions such as lifting and moving heavy items or repetitive manual tasks can be stressful. Occupations most heavily exposed to physical workload are miners, farmers, lumberjacks,

Table 4.1 Sources of stress on jobs

Mechanical
• Vehicles, machinery, equipment in motion, noise
• Tension and compression, vibration
• Pressure and vacuum equipment, firearms
Radiation
• Ionizing ultraviolet
• Infrared radiofrequency
• Electromagnetic field, laser
• Extremely low frequency
Fire and explosion
• Flammable substances, explosives
Temperature
• High-temperature materials, cryogenic fluids
Hazardous environments
• Confined spaces working at heights
• Working at sea
Electrical
• High voltage equipment live electrical equipment
• Static charge
Chemical/hazardous substances
• Carcinogens, corrosive agents
• Irritants and sensitizing agents, toxic substances
• Genotoxins (mutagens, teratogens), solvents
• Atmospheric contaminants (dusts, vapors, fumes, etc.)
Personal
• Working alone, sociological/psychological
• Slips, trips, and falls, fixed posture, e.g., microscopy
• Scientific diving, heat/cold stress
• Repetitive movements, e.g., keyboard, pipetting
• Manual handling including striking and grasping
Biological
• Biological material, allergens
• Biological irritants, genotoxins
Zoonoses
• Handling of large and/or small animals
Other
• Hazardous wastes, human samples

fishermen, construction workers, storage workers, and health care personnel (particularly those caring for the elderly). Repetitive tasks and static muscular load are found in many industrial and service occupations. Most of the factors behind such exposures can be eliminated or minimized through the design of adequate machinery and tools and through automation, mechanization, improvement of ergonomics, better organization of work, and training in appropriate work practices.

A great many people feel that their work is "mentally heavy." Psychological stress caused by time pressure and hectic work has become more prevalent during the past decade. Other work factors that may have adverse psychological effects include heavy responsibility for human or economic concerns, monotonous work or that which requires constant concentration, shiftwork, work under the threat of violence as, for example, police or prison work, and isolated work. Psychological stress and overload have been associated with sleep disturbances, burnout syndromes, and depression. There is also epidemiological evidence of an elevated risk of cardiovascular disorders, particularly coronary heart disease and hypertension. Severe psychological conditions (psychotraumas) may be seen among the workers involved in serious catastrophes or major accidents where human lives are threatened or lost.

In many industrial and service occupations, including health services, irregular working hours and frequent shifts are associated with several physiological and psychosocial problems that affect the health of workers and require exceptional capacity for adaptation. Adaptation to unconventional diurnal rhythms varies widely between individuals.

In terms of specific jobs, there are numerous ones in which there is little contact with others, lonely jobs. Among them are metalworking (machinist, machine tool operator, tool-and-die maker, drill-press operator) and some computer jobs (operators and programmers), among others. Many jobs involve much longer hours than one might expect. Among them are corporate executives, religious occupations (ministers, priests, rabbis), many physicians, and other medical-related personnel, and lawyers and judges.[3]

Highly competitive jobs include photojournalists, newscasters, mayors, professional athletes, people in the fashion world, executives, and politicians, among others. Jobs with very high time pressures (deadlines, quotas, time-sensitive work) include executives, court reporters, air traffic controllers, stockbrokers, stevedores, motion picture editors, technical writers, book authors, and photojournalists, among others.[4]

Physical

Extensive information is available about physical stressors associated with jobs. There are physical hazards and accident risks, chemical hazards, carcinogens, and biological agents.

Mechanical factors, unshielded machinery, unsafe structures, confined spaces, working at heights, working at sea, and using dangerous tools are among the most prevalent physical hazards. Others include noise, vibration, working with extremely high- or low-temperature materials, ionizing and nonionizing radiations, and microclimatic conditions. Between 10 percent and 30 percent of the workforce in industrialized countries and up to 80 percent in developing and newly industrialized countries are exposed to such physical factors, and in some high-risk sectors such as mining, manufacturing, and construction, all workers may be affected. Noise-induced hearing loss is among the most prevalent occupational diseases. Flammable substances present another clear risk to workers in many jobs. In addition, some jobs involve working with or around explosives. There are also numerous jobs that involve electrical risks. Working with high voltage equipment and live electrical equipment presents clear hazards, but static charge can also be a source of danger.

There is an extremely large number of different chemical products in use in modern work environments, and the number is constantly growing. Hazardous exposure to these chemicals is most prevalent in industries processing chemicals and metals, in the manufacture of consumer goods using metal products and plastics, in the production of textiles and artificial fibers, and in the construction industry. In addition, chemicals are increasingly used in virtually all types of work, including nonindustrial activities such as hospital and office work, cleaning, cosmetic and beauty services, and numerous other services. Metal poisoning, solvent damage to the central nervous system and liver, pesticide poisoning, dermal and respiratory allergies, dermatoses, cancers, and reproductive disorders are among the health effects of such exposures.

Some jobs involve potential exposure to carcinogens—chemical (e.g., benzene, chromium, nitrosamines, asbestos), physical (e.g., ultraviolet, ionizing, and other forms of radiation), and biological (e.g., aflatoxins, tumor viruses). The most common cancers resulting from occupational carcinogenic exposures are cancers of the lung, bladder, skin, mesothelium, liver, hematopoietic tissue, bone, and soft connective tissue. Among certain occupational groups, such as asbestos sprayers, occupational cancer may be the leading factor in ill health and mortality.

There are also numerous biological agents, viruses, bacteria, parasites, fungi, molds, and organic dusts that can be hazardous in certain jobs. The hepatitis B and hepatitis C viruses and tuberculosis infections (particularly among health care workers), asthmas (among people exposed to organic dust), and chronic parasitic diseases (particularly among agricultural and forestry workers) are the most common occupational diseases resulting from such exposures. Allergic dermatoses are one of the most prevalent occupational diseases and can lead to incapacity for work and to the need to move the worker to another occupation. The respiratory tract, followed by the skin surface, is the most important route for hazardous agents to enter the body. This makes occupational respiratory diseases the priority problem in any occupational health program. Occupational asthmas are caused by exposure to several organic dusts, microorganisms, bacteria, fungi, and molds, several chemicals, both organic and inorganic. In addition to respiratory allergens, the respiratory system may also be exposed to mineral dusts that cause fibrotic responses and are often associated with an elevated risk of cancer. Pneumoconioses have been found to occur in as many as half of workers most heavily exposed to silica, coal dust, or asbestos fibers.

In terms of physical demands on the job, "office" and "professional" jobs usually are lowest—statisticians, mathematicians, actuaries, consultants, and the like. The highest, on the other hand, involve those who work outside and professional athletes. There are, however, numerous white-collar jobs that are physically demanding—veterinarians, surgeons, and osteopaths; musicians and conductors; and photojournalists, among others. Likewise, there are numerous blue-collar jobs that have very low physical demands—bus drivers, guards and correction officers, repairers, and assemblers, among others.[5]

Role

The role you are expected to play on the job can also cause stress. A role is a set of expected behaviors associated with a position in a group or organization. Stress can result from either role ambiguity or role conflict that people can experience in groups. For example, an employee who is feeling pressure from her boss to work longer hours while also being asked by her family for more time at home will almost certainly experience stress. Similarly, a new employee experiencing role ambiguity because of poor orientation and training practices by the organization will also suffer from stress.

Many types of work, such as seafaring, transport, and supervision of prisons, may require longer shifts or longer periods to be spent at the workplace than the regular eight hours per day. In extreme cases, such periods at the worksite may be several months. In such special conditions, the place of living and place of work are the same, which creates specific environmental and psychosocial problems and needs. Such workplaces may increase in number in the future since mining, forestry, and oil exploitation activities, for example, are moving increasingly to remote areas. Offshore oil and gas drilling are constantly expanding and moving further from the shore. Underwater mining may become a major source of ores in the future.

Interpersonal Stressors

Interpersonal stressors are those associated with relationships that confront people in organizations. For example, group pressures regarding the restriction of output and norm conformity can lead to stress. Leadership style may also cause stress. Employees who feel a strong need to participate in decision making may feel stress if their boss refuses to allow participation. And individuals with conflicting personalities may experience stress if required to work too closely together. A person with an internal locus of control might be frustrated when working with someone who prefers to wait and just let things happen.

Several social aspects of work may raise health concerns; for example, the gender distribution and segregation of jobs and equality at the workplace, social relationships between managers and employees, and social support from fellow workers are aspects of work that may enrich or reduce social contacts. In many services and public jobs, the social pressure from customers, clients, or the public may cause additional psychological workload. Working conditions, type of work, vocational and professional status, and geographical location of the workplace and employment also have a profound impact on the social status and social well-being of working people.

The special occupational health problems of working women are receiving attention. Heavy physical work, the double work burden of job and family, less developed working methods, and traditional social roles are the factors that increase the burden of female workers. The design of machinery and work tools are often made according to male anthropometry, although female workers use such equipment. In many service occupations, female workers may be exposed to the threat of violence from clients or to sexual harassment from fellow workers. Women may also face problems of occupational exposures to physical hazards that are hazardous to reproductive health (including infertility in both sexes, spontaneous abortions, fetal death, teratogenesis, fetal cancer, fetotoxicity, or retarded development of the fetus or the newborn). Both male and female workers may be affected by occupational hazards, but particular concern should be paid by women of fertile age and during pregnancy.

Consequences

Just as stress itself can be positive or negative, the results of stress may be positive or negative. The negative consequences may be physiological, psychological, behavioral, and/or medical.

The body has natural responses to stress (known as the fight or flight response). Those responses include cardiovascular (e.g., raised blood pressure, diversion of blood from the intestines to the muscle tissue in preparation for action), biochemical (e.g., the release of cortisone for allergy protection, sugars for extra energy, and natural pain killers), gastrointestinal (e.g., indigestion), and musculoskeletal (shoulder and neck pain) reactions. Signs indicating that stress is becoming negative include general irritability; rapid pulse or pounding heart; dryness of the throat and mouth; impulsiveness; emotional instability; increased perspiration from hands, underarms, and forehead; tightening of the forehead and jaws;

inability to concentrate; fatigue; uneasiness; anxiety; tensing of shoulders and neck muscles; feeling of being all keyed up; and insomnia.

Your perception of the situation determines your response and your level of stress. What is stressful to you might not be to someone else. Psychological consequences of stress interfere with your mental health and well-being. Psychological stress often occurs when you perceive that a task or assignment might exceed your capabilities or that necessary resources for successfully completing the task are not available. Typical psychological stress responses include depression, anxiety, difficulty in concentrating, short-term memory loss, job dissatisfaction, sleep disturbances, depression, family problems, and sexual dysfunction.[6] There is a difference between work behavior and personalities, and attitudes. Work behavior is what is expected of you when you are employed, and it can be modified and measured. Personalities and attitudes are more difficult to measure and assess, so organizations typically concentrate on behavior.

Work behavior is a very powerful tool for judging if an individual may be suffering from stress; it can be observed, measured, and compared to existing norms and standards. Some workplace behaviors that may indicate that a person is experiencing stress include accident proneness, inability to complete tasks, working unusually long hours, continually working through normal work breaks, observable mood swings, accumulation of excessive flextime, out of character negative comments about work, long breaks, late start, early finish, disruptive to and/or frequent conflicts with others, and withdrawal from the workgroup. In addition, stress may lead to detrimental or harmful actions, such as smoking, alcoholism, overeating, and drug abuse.

Negative stress also has direct consequences for organizations. For an operating employee, stress may translate into poor quality work and lower productivity. For a manager, stress may mean faulty decision making and disruptions in working relationships. Withdrawal behaviors can also result from stress. People who are having difficulties with stress in their jobs are more likely to call in sick or to leave the organization. More subtle forms of withdrawal may also occur. A manager may start missing deadlines, for example, or taking longer lunch breaks. Employees may also withdraw by developing feelings of indifference. The irritation displayed by people under great stress can make them difficult to get along with. Job satisfaction, morale, and commitment can all suffer as a result of excessive levels of stress. So, too, can the motivation to perform.

Medical consequences of stress affect an individual's physiological well-being. Heart disease and stroke have been linked to stress, as have headaches, backaches, ulcers, and related disorders, and skin conditions such as acne and hives. Yet another consequence of stress is burnout—a feeling of exhaustion that may develop when someone experiences too much stress for an extended period of time. Burnout results in constant fatigue, frustration, and helplessness. Increased rigidity follows, as does a loss of self-confidence and psychological withdrawal. The individual dreads going to work, often puts in long hours but gets less accomplished than before, and exhibits signs of mental and physical exhaustion.

Managing Stress

You should be concerned with stress. Indeed, all organizations and individuals should be concerned with stress. Such concerns have led to the development of numerous approaches to help manage stress.[7]

Well-managed organizations try to eliminate physical and psychological stressors by modifying the work environment and work organization and, if necessary, by changing managerial systems. Prevention and control include participation, training, and education, the introduction of stress management methods for individuals at risk, and psychological support from managers, fellow workers, and occupational health services. In the case of the threat of violence, measures for eliminating the likelihood of such hazards (e.g., working in pairs instead of working alone) and provision of adequate protective structures and equipment for cases of emergency will improve worker confidence and reduce stress.

Many organizations now sponsor wellness programs. Some have adopted stress management programs, health promotion programs, and other kinds of programs for this purpose. They commonly include exercise-related activities as well as classroom instruction dealing with smoking cessation, weight reduction, and general stress management. Some companies have a gym on-site, and still, others negotiate discounted health club membership rates with local establishments.

Accidents as a source of stress are, for the most part, preventable. Organizations that acknowledge this try to provide safe and healthy work environments, working practices, and safety systems. They may also employ behavioral and management practices designed to reduce accident rates.

You need to learn to handle your own stress, too. Effective stress prevention often means leading a balanced life and looking after yourself. If you are in reasonably good physical health, you can cope with pressure better than if you are not. You need to watch your diet, exercise and relax. A healthy diet is essential to maintain the body in good condition. Foods should be selected from all the main groups, in particular, food from the plant groups, including vegetables, fruits, grains, and pastas. These foods provide fiber, which helps to keep the body healthy. Regular exercise is important to keep the body systems functioning in good order. You should exercise for 30 minutes, three times per week. The type of exercise is not as important as long as there is some light puffing involved. Taking regular breaks from the job actually invigorates the body and mind. These breaks can range from 10 minutes, lunch break, weekends, to annual leave. They are essential to your well-being.

You should also learn to monitor your own body to tell when it is telling you that you are under too much pressure. You should have some idea what your resting pulse rate is and what it is after a reasonable workout. You should know your blood pressure. When is your peak energy level during the day? You should have some understanding of what events cause you the most stress. Identifying the source(s) of stress is very important. Knowing the source will help you cope with the stress.

Coping with Stress

You can cope with stress in general or focus on specific stressors. As just indicated, general approaches include diet, exercise, and relaxation. Focusing on specific stressors will provide faster relief, however. You will have to approach your supervisor and colleagues if the stressors exist at work.

You can also use time management to control stress. The idea behind time management is that many daily pressures can be reduced or eliminated if individuals do a better job of managing time. One approach to time management is to make a list every morning of the things to be done that day (a "To Do" list). The items on the list are then grouped into three categories based on importance priority: critical activities that must be performed, important activities that should be performed, and optional or trivial things that can be postponed or given to someone else. Then you do things on the list in their order of importance.

Finally, you can manage stress through support groups. A support group can be as simple as a group of family members or friends to enjoy leisure time with. Going out after work with a couple of coworkers to a basketball game or a movie, for example, can help relieve stress built up during the day. Family and friends can help you cope with stress on an ongoing basis and during times of crisis. You also may use more formal support groups at community centers or religious institutions.

Information to Seek

Just as you should seek information about accidents and safety for any job for which you are interested, you should also seek information about stressors and the level of stress on those jobs. Some of the questions you may wish to seek answers to are the following.

- Does the company have a wellness program?
- Does the company have an employee assistance program?
- What is the level of turnover on this job?
- What are the major sources of stress on this job?
- What are the normal working conditions for this job?
- Does this job involve ever having to handle or be exposed to chemicals, biological agents, or the like?
- Does this job involve ever having to come into contact with people who are known to be sick?

Chapter Takeaways

- Stress can be positive or negative.
- Multiple causes of stress including task, role, and interpersonal.

- Results can be positive or negative.
- Different ways of managing/coping with stress.
- EAPs—employee assistance programs.

Think About This Chapter Again

Look over the notes you took before reading this chapter. What changes would you make now?

Think about these anecdotes in relation to this chapter.

"As a jobless 24-year-old in 2008 who had to move back home and had tattoos and piercings, I had to cover up and take out the metal.

I went on one interview that was at a business professional-type place, and everything seemed to be going well. Three interviews in, everything was still smooth, when the old woman asked if I had any tattoos or piercings. I thought that was pretty personal, and while I was vague with my answers, I told her that yes, I had some piercings done, but took them out. She actually stood up, asked me to stand up, and got right into my face. I did have some scaring from a lip ring and several nose rings, and she was looking at me so mean at that point that I told her I felt uncomfortable. She said, 'Well, with the scars, we won't hire you.' OK, BYE! I got a job a week later anyway, but damn … that was really weird. And that company ended up shutting down 5 years later, so screw 'em."

Source: Adopted from www.buzzfeed.com/jessg/wildest-and-most-frustrating-job -interviews

---

"I like to think there's no such thing as messing up a job interview, only practical learning. My grand realization came after a group interview. I was interviewing to be a Red Bull girl, so I guess you could consider it more of an audition. Unfortunately, I didn't realize that at the time. The interviewer assigned us a task to work on as a group, and I took it way too seriously.

In retrospect, clearly, they wanted to observe how we interacted with one another, how 'bubbly' we were, and how well we would fit as a brand ambassador. But instead, my priority was being the best at the task to the detriment of everything else. I didn't get the job and it didn't take me long to work out why."

Source: Adopted from https://fashionjournal.com.au/life/job-interview-blunder/

Recommended Reading

The following could expand your understanding of the chapter's material:

Aldwin, C. M. 2007. *Stress Coping and Development—An Integrative Perspective.* The Guilford Press.
Cooper, Cary, L., and P. Dewe. 2004. *Stress: A Brief History*, Blackwell Publishing.
Patmore, A. 2006. *The Truth about Stress.* Atlantic Books.

CHAPTER 5

Poor Management

Make some notes of what you expect in this chapter. Write down what you feel are examples of poor management. Keep that in mind as you read this chapter.

One of the most important things to be aware of in seeking a safe job is the managers of the organization and especially any manager with whom you will closely interact. In general, poor managers or bad bosses do not believe in participative management and won't involve you in any decisions. Typically, they will not involve those who are not managers in decision making or even ask them for suggestions or their ideas. Bad bosses tend to overuse their power and may even be rude to employees. They may even be crude in interactions with others in and outside the organization. They don't seem to understand that failing to hire or losing good employees is not a good thing for the organization; they seem to feel that anyone can easily be replaced without lowering productivity or morale.

The quality of management has long been known to be a powerful force shaping the attitudes and behavior of those in the organization. Good managers can help obtain good behavior and performance. Poor managers, on the other hand, help to bring about poor behavior and inferior performance. In addition, the way managers treat employees and handle complaints about poor performance affects workers' attitudes toward their coworkers as well as toward the job itself. Sometimes, poor managers simply reflect the behavior of top managers, who set the tone for the entire organization. For example, the manager may simply be carrying out company policies and rules—written, spoken, or implied by upper management's behavior. Furthermore, in matters such as pay raises and promotions, the organization's policies specify what can and cannot be done to reward employees.

Managers have power in organizations so that they can perform their functions but it is easy for them to abuse that power, especially when they feel either too superior or too inferior. Those who feel they are the privileged elite in the organization may abuse their power in an effort to remind themselves and others of their stature. Those who feel inferior may abuse their power because they fear losing control or because acting that way is the only way they can feel superior.

Virtually all research and practical experience suggests that using coercive, punishing practices is not effective management. The adage says, "You can catch more flies with honey than with vinegar," but it does not mean that managers should overlook poor performance; rather, it merely advises that considerate and professional feedback, along with proper training and resources, will yield better results than abusive techniques will. Many of the specific examples of these poor managers or bad bosses are shown in the following figure, which suggests the explosive situation brought about by their behavior.

BAD BOSSES:
EXAMPLES OF MISMANAGEMENT

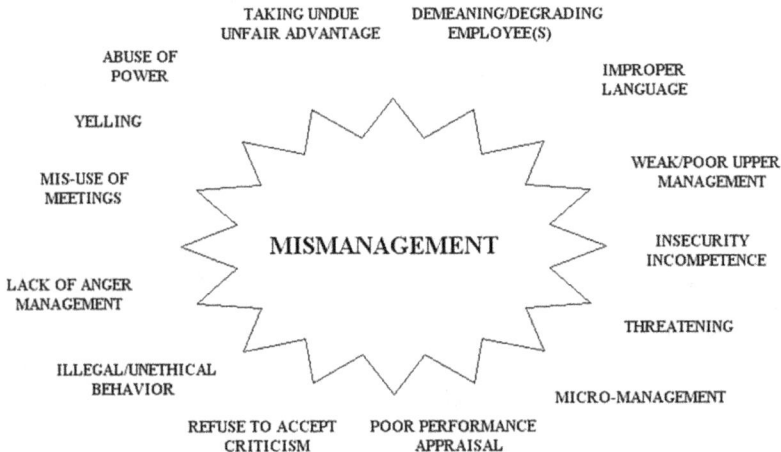

Hopefully, you will think that these are unusual, leading you to say, "Surely no one would actually do that!" Disappointingly, though, these are all real examples from research and surveys taken from everyday life in organizations in the United States (one wonders if examples from around the world would be similar). Even if you are not familiar with them, you should be aware of them as you search for a safe job.

Successful business people don't get ahead by wishing they had someone else's job title, corner office, company car, or market share. They get ahead the mundane way, by doing more and doing it better. Envy is a monster with a gluttonous appetite. And it's never satisfied. Pursue your goals, not someone else's goals.

—*James Dale*

Factors of Which to Be Aware

Poor managers may be thought of as falling into one or more of the following categories—authoritarianism, narcissism, abusive supervision, unpredictability, or Machiavellianism.[1] Or they may be narcissistic, bipolar, psychopathic, and obsessive-compulsive.[2] Whatever classification is used in more detail will better equip you to recognize many of these. These are based on Van Fleet and Van Fleet.[3]

- **Bosses Who Threaten Employees**—Like those who ride horses and crack their whips, many bosses threaten employees in the hope that their scare tactics will elicit the desired behavior so that it will be unnecessary to do anything more. Other bosses use threats to remind the employee that they are the boss—that they have this power and are not afraid to use it.
- **Bosses Who Take Undue or Unfair Advantage**—Using their positions in the organization, bosses take advantage of situations that should benefit their employees and their organizations. In the hands of bad bosses, however, that power sometimes is used to gain undue or unfair advantage.
- **Bosses Who Are Heavy-Handed in Other Ways**—In addition to the above examples, bad bosses find other ways to abuse their power. The reasons may be as varied as the tactics—to hold back a too-competent employee, bad chemistry between the boss and

employee, to satisfy a need for control in the boss's psyche, to pattern after a parent or former employer, or even to persuade an employee to resign.

- **Bosses Who Do Not Control Their Anger**—Some bosses are ill-fitted for management because they either have not learned to manage their anger or have learned to express their anger inappropriately in a controlling, threatening way. Their anger creates a highly emotional state that results in a great many problems for them and subsequently for those who interact with them. Bad bosses resort to such tactics as angry outbursts or tantrums, loud voices, negative body language, the use of offensive language, and other means of demeaning or degrading employees. Attempts to communicate while in a highly emotional state are likely to miss the mark.

- **Bosses Who Yell at Employees**—Many bosses tend to raise their voices unnecessarily and yell when they are overly stressed or when something meets their disapproval. For some, yelling is merely a habit. Oddly enough, a fairly large proportion of managers believe that they must yell in order to prove their authority. They obviously never bought into the first part of "speak softly but carry a big stick."

- **Bosses Who Display Angry Outbursts and Tantrums**—Sadly, some bosses go even further than yelling at their employees by displaying angry outbursts or tantrums. Such behavior can genuinely frighten employees to the point where it not only interferes with their happiness and productivity at work but also carries over into their life after work leading to unnecessary family stress. They spend as much time thinking about the incidents and dreading the next one as they do in carrying out the tasks for which they are hired and paid.

- **Bosses Who Use Offensive Language**—As noted above, some managers yell, scream, and throw things when angry or upset. Some also use offensive language when communicating with employees. While this is unprofessional and unnecessary, for employees who are opposed to foul language, this managerial practice is especially offensive and degrading.

- **Bosses Who Belittle, Demean, or Degrade Employees—** Yelling, having temper tantrums, and using foul language are generally viewed as demeaning or degrading; but some bad bosses find even more ways to achieve the same improper task, including illegal and/or unethical behavior. On too many occasions, examples of illegal or unethical behavior seem to fill the pages of newspapers and magazines. For the most part, those are unusual, extreme incidents, but such behavior on a much smaller scale also occurs far more frequently than anyone would wish.

- **Bosses Who Micromanage—**Over-controlling or micromanaging has long been identified as a sign of weak or poor management. Often it results from a lack of self-confidence on the part of the boss; in other cases, it results from the boss's lack of trust in employees. Micromanaging isn't merely annoying to employees; it lowers morale and performance on the job. Micromanagers love their power and use it whenever possible, especially by requiring their personal approval before an employee can act. They seem to firmly believe that any type of work break (lunch, rest, bathroom, or whatever) reduces productivity. They tend to employ deadlines for everything, no matter how minor.

- **Bosses Who Provide Poor Performance Appraisal—**Managers are responsible for providing employee feedback about how well employees are achieving their functions. Without that feedback, employees cannot know how well they are performing their jobs. They probably won't improve in weak areas if they are not shown them. They may not continue effective performance if they are not sure that it is effective. Even though there are numerous training programs, software packages, and even Internet sites to assist managers in conducting performance appraisals and providing feedback, some bosses don't do it very well.

- **Bosses Who Use Meetings Inappropriately—**Meetings should serve as important activities within organizations. Meetings enable information to be exchanged among several participants at the same time thus enabling efficient communication within the organization. They are important to the efficient operation of organizations as they facilitate upward as well as downward and lateral flows of information. However, meetings can be dysfunctional if used as an improper means of giving performance feedback or if incorrect information is shared.

- **Bosses Who Try to Cover Up Their Insecurity and/or Incompetence**—Employees don't seem to get bent out of shape if their boss doesn't know all the answers, or how to perform some of the tasks that the workers perform. What they dislike is a boss who tries to cover up the fact that he or she is insecure or incompetent. "Because I'm the boss" is not an acceptable response to workers' questions. They want a boss who acknowledges a lack of information or skills but then does something about it. Similarly, they lose respect for a boss who cannot make decisions. After all, that's high on the list of the things managers are paid to do. Nor do they respect bosses who surround themselves with "yes" employees and refuse to accept blame or criticism.
- **Bosses Who Avoid Making Decisions**—Avoiding decisions that could and should be made is a sure way of demonstrating incompetence or insecurity. Problems do not get solved in a timely manner when a boss is avoiding making decisions.
- **Bosses Who Cannot Accept Criticism**—Without the knowledge of what others perceive as incorrect behavior, people can't modify their behavior to do what is perceived as correct behavior. Being open to criticism is an important characteristic of good managers. Regrettably, some managers can't seem to accept criticism.

There are, of course, other examples of poor managers or bad bosses such as threatening an employee to accept work assignments beyond his or her job description, forcing workers to work overtime, threatening to relocate an employee, demanding personal work on company time, misleading or overstating a problem to motivate an employee, treating employees as if they were children, touching improperly to intimidate a person of a different race or culture, making false accusations to support low-performance ratings. Of course, identifying these or others while seeking a job is not easy. Any job may be better than no job and so you may not be too fussy in the first place. In addition, managers tend to put on their "best faces" during job search processes so "what you see" may well not be "what you get." So, what can you do to try to identify these poor managers before you accept a job offer?

Information to Seek While Searching for a Job

First, try to talk to others who work for the prospective boss, even the former jobholder if possible. Do your homework and ask questions. Doing your homework means trying to find out about the organization and those who are employed there. One of the best sources is the Internet, which usually can be accessed from a public library. Check the organization's website, dig deeply, and read the press releases. There are sites where people can complain about organizations. See if the organization you are considering is on any of them and what is said. Be careful, however, as many of these sites do not screen the individuals to determine if they have legitimate complaints.

Have questions that you want to ask them as well. Not just about the job, pay, and benefits, but about the supervision and its impact. How long do people usually stay in the job? In the organization? Are there opportunities for upward evaluations and feedback? Does the company use 360° feedback for its supervisors and managers? Is there a grievance process and/or are ombudspersons available? These sorts of questions will help you understand the organization and its managers as much as you can before accepting a job.

If possible, try to spend time at the organization before accepting a job. Visit the organization and preferably the actual job site. Watch how people act and listen to what break or lunch conversations are about. See if you can informally ask about what people think of their bosses, the company in general, and its culture. Maybe you can ask if anyone knows of any kind of personal emergency a coworker has had and how the boss and the organization responded to that emergency. Maybe it wasn't an emergency but merely childbirth or a prolonged illness. How bosses and organizations respond to unusual events can also suggest a great deal about what your life would be like should you accept a job at the organization.

Once you get to an interview, the information available to you changes. How do the organization and the individual(s) involved handle the interview process? Are they willing to accommodate your schedule and needs or do they assign you a time and say, "Take it or leave it?" Do you get the impression that you are just a number or "one of the pack" or do they treat you as an individual with genuine interest? These impressions can reveal a lot about the organization and its willingness to tolerate bad bosses. Be alert to how you are handled during the process.

With that in mind, you should also evaluate the people you meet and the process itself. Who are the people you meet? Are they all alike (same race, same-sex, same organization level, same department, same everything)? If they are, that may suggest aspects of the organization that you may or may not like. Is everyone asking the same questions? If so, they may be so suspicious that no one can deviate from a predetermined set—that may not be the kind of organization that you want to work for. What are the questions you are being asked? Are any of them inappropriate and too personal— marital status; children, present or planned; spouse employed; and the like? If they are, you may want to think twice before accepting a position in that organization.

Chapter Takeaways

- Quality of management is a powerful force.
- Numerous examples of poor managers.
- Do homework about the organization.

Think About This Chapter Again

Look over the notes you took before reading this chapter. What changes would you make now?

Think about these anecdotes in relation to this chapter.

> "I landed my first job by embracing persistence and networking. Fresh out of college, I attended a local tech meet-up where a chance conversation with a seasoned developer led to an internship opportunity. I worked hard, asked questions, and showed genuine interest in

learning. Within a few months, that internship turned into a full-time position. This experience taught me the value of putting myself out there and seizing opportunities, no matter how small they seem."

Source: Adopted from https://careerconnectors.org/how-did-you-get-your-first-job -15-real-life-stories/

"I've been working in the media industry since 2021. I'm currently working as a news writer, but I've also been an editor and researcher. In my experience, being on the job hunt is just as stressful and labor-intensive as having an actual nine-to-five, except without the sole benefit of getting paid.

My last job—my dream job, might I add—unfortunately, ended suddenly in redundancy and I saw myself frantically applying to anything and everything that I might be even just slightly qualified for. Looking for a new job is always a bit daunting and I won't lie and say I wasn't in a pretty bad emotional state (I was genuinely heartbroken). I was properly searching for about two to three months before I managed to land something, which is surprisingly quick knowing that it can take as long as a whole year before something picks up.

I landed my current job the old-fashioned way: by scouring for anything remotely in my field online and sending my resume absolutely everywhere. I feel very lucky that I managed to find something that actually interests me and that I'm surrounded by great team members.

If you're currently in the trenches, remember that it's okay to feel downhearted and upset about not landing a job yet. Unemployment is the pits, even without the looming threat of a cost-of-living crisis breathing down our necks. I would say that the one thing that got me going is knowing that countless other people have experienced this same situation and that a job isn't all you are.

Redundancies, being let go, or choosing to quit a job isn't easy, but I promise it isn't the end of the world! It's easier said than done but keeping your eyes and ears open for any opportunities, even if it's in a different field or role that you're used to, is the sure-fire way of getting

somewhere. Adding some of your own personality into your cover letter and interview is also a great way of getting noticed. Don't just think
about what the employer wants to hear, find some way to incorporate
yourself into the application."

Source: Adopted from https://fashionjournal.com.au/life/positive-job-hunt/

Recommended Reading

The following could expand your understanding of the chapter's material:

Savas, O. 2019. "Impact of Dysfunctional Leadership on Organizational Perfor-
mance." *Global Journal of Management and Business Research* 19 (1): 37–41.
Erikson, T. 2021. *Surrounded by Bad Bosses (and Lazy Employees): How to
Stop Struggling, Start Succeeding, and Deal with Idiots at Work.* St. Martin's
Essentials.
Van Fleet, E. W., and D. D. Van Fleet. 2007. *Workplace Survival: Dealing with
Bad Bosses, Bad Workers, Bad Jobs.* Publish America.

CHAPTER 6

Workplace Violence

Make some notes of what you expect in this chapter. Write down what you feel are examples of workplace violence. Keep that in mind as you read this chapter.

Factors of Which to Be Aware

When life at work results in more stress than support, employees and managers alike can expect to face increasing incidents of interpersonal conflicts and workplace violence.[1] Some events contribute to such stress, including offshoring, outsourcing, reorganizing, reengineering, budget-cutting, downsizing, and just-in-time delivery.[2] Bad workplaces, bad jobs, bad managers, and bad coworkers can lead to an organization's potential for violence.

In the United States workplace violence started in the late 1970s when American businesspeople were kidnapped in several South American countries and held for ransom. Then during the 1980s, Americans working abroad were kidnapped in Lebanon for political purposes. But what most people would consider workplace violence occurred on August 19, 1986, when a postal employee in Edmond, Oklahoma, shot 14 former coworkers and himself because of the way he had been disciplined the previous day. This incident gave rise to the expression "going postal" and may well have been the beginning of the use of lethal weapons as tools of workplace violence in the United States.

As shown in the figure below, workplace violence is related to other forms of violence. When seeking to find a safe job, it is the form that is of the greatest concern and so, you should concentrate on it.

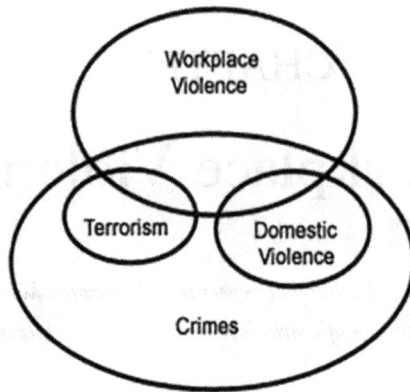

Source: Van Fleet, D. D., and E. W. Van Fleet. 2010. *The Violence Volcano: Reducing the Threat of Workplace Violence*. Information Age Publishing, p. 44.

Information to Seek While Searching for a Job

Does the job involve any of the following (based on Nater et al.[3]):

- Working and traveling in known high-crime areas
- Working with customers or the public, particularly when exchanging money with the public—cashiers, convenience store attendants, taxi drivers
- Any situation in which money or valuables are handled
- Handling prescription drugs—pharmacists, veterinarians
- Working alone or in small groups—store clerks, real estate agents
- Working in isolated or low traffic areas—isolated reception area, washrooms, storage areas, utility rooms
- Carrying out inspection or enforcement duties—inspectors, assessors
- Providing service, care, advice, or education—health care workers, social workers, teachers
- Working in health care, such as nurses and medical assistants
- Working with mentally unstable or volatile persons—mental health workers

- Working where alcohol is served—bartenders, food, and beverage staff
- Any situation where individuals might be under the influence of drugs or alcohol
- Working in a mobile workplace—taxicab, bus driver, salesperson
- Working during periods of intense organizational change or turmoil—downsizing, reorganization, strikes
- Working with third-party workers, such as contractors or subcontractors
- Areas with poor lighting—corridors, parking lots, offices, stairs
- Environments with the presence of firearms
- Delivery services—post office, UPS, FedEx
- Transporting or moving patients in health care
- Situations with high worker turnover
- Working late at night or early in the morning
- Areas with inadequate security
- Working in high-crime areas—bars, banks, financial companies
- Situations with no or poor emergency communication
- Environments in which staff lack training on violence prevention skills and inadequate safety policies
- Areas where vision may be blocked or there are no escape routes

This list is not intended to be comprehensive. Individuals working in these sorts of situations are more likely to experience workplace violence. As indicated previously, custodial care in mental health occupations, technical and industrial schools, corrections officers, security guards, and bartenders are occupations with high rates of workplace violence.

You should also check the sources in the Appendix A to this chapter for any information that might suggest the organization could be the target of workplace violence.

Don't be afraid to go out on a limb. That's where the fruit is.
—H. Jackson Browne

Questions to Ask in Interviewing

There is a website that provides excellent questions.[4] Among those most pertinent to finding out about the organization's potential or lack thereof for workplace violence are:

- Ask to see the organization's safety plan.
- How do people react to one another during the course of your interview or a site visit?
- What does a typical day or week look like in this role?
- Are there opportunities for advancement within the company?
- How long have you been with the company?
- Has your role changed since you've been here?
- Why did you come to this company?
- What's your favorite part about working here?
- What are the company's most important values?
- How does the company ensure it is upholding its values?
- What's the typical leadership style here?
- Who will I report to directly?
- How would you describe the work environment here—is the work typically more collaborative or more independent?
- Does anyone at the company or on this team hang out outside the office?

Chapter Takeaways

- Workplace violence is happening.
- There are lots of contributing factors.
- Numerous sources help identify potential situations where it may occur.

Think About This Chapter Again

Look over the notes you took before reading this chapter. What changes would you make now?

Think about these anecdotes in relation to this chapter.

> "It was 200x, and I was living at home and desperate for a job. I found an ad, and after a brief phone screening, was told to show up the next day prepared for an all-day interview with no other details provided. I went and was told that they sold office supplies door-to-door at local businesses and that I'd be riding with one of their salesmen out in the field for the entire day. I hopped into a raggedy Honda Civic with a complete stranger, and my fears were validated on our very first stop. He tried to get an appointment with the owner of the business and became so aggressive with the secretary that she became visibly uncomfortable and told us to leave. The only commonality I remember establishing with him in the five hours we were together was the fact we had both seen the Lord of the Rings movies. They offered me the job in a way that tried to make it seem like they didn't take anyone off the street (they clearly did), and I turned it down."
>
> *Source:* Adopted from www.buzzfeed.com/jessg/wildest-and-most-frustrating-job-interviews

> "The job hunt for my current role coincided with me moving abroad from A to M, so looking back it was a pretty emotionally turbulent time, with so much change in my life. I resigned from my previous role at *Ensemble Magazine* about a month before moving to Australia, so I was job hunting while looking for a place to live, writing a few stories freelance, and working on a makeup website.
>
> I was applying for all kinds of vaguely fashion and beauty-related communication roles in major cities. A few interviews at magazines and PR agencies went well and were offered to me but ultimately, they didn't align with my experience or values. I didn't feel like I was 'starting from scratch' but I also could've backed myself and applied for more senior roles. I was searching for about two months in total, I felt stressed the entire time.
>
> A friend who worked at *Fashion Journal* let me know about an assistant editor role coming up, so I organized my portfolio and cover

letter and applied as soon as it went up. While I was in that city scoping out other prospects, I interviewed for the role but didn't get it. When I found out I was devastated! But a few weeks later, the person who interviewed me called to say a features editor role was coming up and asked if I'd be interested. This felt more aligned with my skills and experience, so of course I said yes, and then I had to convince my boyfriend that city M was way cooler than city S anyway.

The job hunt is such an emotional rollercoaster. Having your skills, talent, and experience constantly questioned and compared is tiring. My advice is to make sure you don't let it question your self-worth; the best opportunities are all about timing. Do the best that you can, then go have fun with your friends and talk about something else. I'd also suggest hitting up your connections, even if they're acquaintances. That's how you'll find out if a role is coming up or who to talk to that might give you an edge when you apply for a role."

Source: Adopted from https://fashionjournal.com.au/life/positive-job-hunt/

Recommended Reading

The following could expand your understanding of the chapter's material:

Denenberg, R. V., and M. Braverman. 1999. *The Violence-Prone Workplace*. Cornell University Press.

Kinney, J. A. 1995. *Violence at Work*. Prentice-Hall.

Nater, F., D. D. Van Fleet, and E. W. Van Fleet. 2023. *Combating Workplace Violence: Creating and Maintaining Safe Work Environments*. Information Age Publishing.

Van Fleet, E. W., and D. D. Van Fleet. 2014. *Violence at Work: What Everyone Should Know*. Information Age Publishing.

CHAPTER 7

Terrorism

Make some notes of what you expect in this chapter. Write down what you feel are examples of terrorism that could impact organizations. Keep that in mind as you read this chapter.

Increasingly terrorist attacks against organizations are occurring. Explosions, kidnapping, hijacking, and other forms of terrorism are becoming all too common events in organizational life. As part of your job search, you should recognize the reality of terrorism impacting organizations. You should have some understanding of terrorism and what organizations may be able to do to reduce the threat of attack. Consider a few relatively recent events.[1]

Events

The Oklahoma City Bombing

At 9:02 a.m. on Wednesday, April 19, 1995, a bomb exploded outside the Alfred P. Murrah Federal Building in Oklahoma City, Oklahoma. An orange-red fireball engulfed the area demolishing the north side of the building and sending shockwaves that were felt 30 miles away. Glass and debris rained down over a sizable area, parking meters and signs were ripped from the ground, and the roofs of nearby buildings collapsed. The blast was estimated to have been caused by 2,000 to 4,000 lb of explosives. It left a crater 30 ft in diameter and 8 ft deep in Northwest Fifth Street. The Murrah Building was not the only building damaged. Others were the Regency Towers, the Oklahoma Water Resources Board building, the Journal Record Building, the YMCA and Day Care Center, the First Methodist Church, and St. Joseph's Old Cathedral.

Survivors staggered from the building, many with their clothes shredded, dripping blood, dazed, and confused. In total, 168 people, including many children at a daycare center, did not survive. Because the whole side of the building collapsed, some occupants on all nine floors were killed or injured as they fell to the bottom of the badly damaged building. Occupants of the building consisted of numerous government agencies including the Department of Defense; U.S. Army Recruiting; Veterans Administration; Drug Enforcement Administration; Secret Service; and the Bureau of Alcohol, Tobacco, and Firearms.

April 19 was apparently not a random date for the bombing. On April 19, 1775, the American Revolutionary War began. On April 19, 1992, the FBI raided the homestead of a militia leader in Ruby Ridge, Idaho. April 19, 1993, was the date on which the "siege at Waco" ended. April 19, 1995, was the date when a member of a White separatist's group was executed for having murdered a Jewish businessman and a Black policeman. April 19, 1993, was the date of issuance indicated on a forged South Dakota driver's license in the possession of Timothy McVeigh when he rented a Ryder Truck north of Oklahoma City in Junction City, Kansas. Only 92 minutes after the explosion, an Oklahoma Highway Patrolman stopped him for speeding and having no license plates on his car. The Patrolman noticed a gun in a shoulder holster and arrested McVeigh for possession of a loaded semiautomatic pistol.

New York World Trade Center Bombing

On February 26, 1993, at approximately noon, terrorists struck the heart of the largest city in the United States. A large homemade boom, concealed in a vehicle, was detonated in an underground garage at the 110-story New York World Trade Center. One of the terrorists responsible, when subsequently captured, admitted the attackers intended to collapse one or both of the twin towers. Had they been successful, they would have killed tens of thousands of innocent people. The terrorists who bombed the World Trade Center succeeded in murdering six innocent people, injuring 1,000 others, and trapping terrified schoolchildren in a smoke-filled elevator for hours.

Two terrorists suspected in this bombing fled the United States immediately following the incident. One was believed to have gone into hiding in Iraq. Both were indicted and immediately following their indictments, a massive international manhunt for the two fugitives was launched by the United States. Wanted posters offering rewards of up to $2 million for information leading to their capture were distributed in a variety of languages. Leaflets printed in several languages were also sent throughout the world. Even matchbooks containing photos of the fugitives were distributed. Almost two years after the bombing, one of the suspects was captured in Pakistan thanks to information provided through the Rewards for Justice Program.

Operation Desert Storm

As Operation Desert Storm began, an East Asian citizen notified the United States that Iraq intended to launch a series of terrorist attacks. The terrorists had surveyed targets; acquired weapons and high explosives; and were ready to move when the United States was notified. The individual's information proved essential in stopping the planned attacks. Had the attacks succeeded, scores of innocent victims from several countries would have been murdered. The informant and the informant's immediate family were provided safety in the United States and a reward.

Amtrak Wreck

In the early morning hours of October 9, 1995, the 12-car Amtrak "Sunset Limited," bound from Miami to Los Angeles, derailed in Hyder, Arizona. There were 248 people on board. The first eight cars left the track, killing one Amtrak employee and injuring more than 100 passengers. Indications are that the railroad tracks had been tampered with and the derailment was not an accident. The Federal Bureau of Investigation is investigating the Arizona train wreck as a criminal matter. These events are but a few that could be discussed. They are not intended to be a representative sample nor necessarily indicative of what is or could occur. Rather, these events are intended to capture your attention and to bring home the urgency of terrorism as a concern in modern organizations.

Concepts

Terrorism refers to a premeditated intent to create fear among many for the purpose of furthering the perpetrator's own views or cause. Terrorists generally are young and well educated and are "middle- or upper-class idealists, who for some reason or other, feel they can change the world for the better by getting rid of the capitalists. These terrorists usually come from good families with parents who are doctors, lawyers, engineers, or some other kind of professionals. [And they] are usually well educated."

An obstacle may be either a steppingstone or a stumbling block.
—Anonymous

Types of Terrorists

There are five types of terrorists. Political terrorists and religious fanatics, average citizen turned terrorist, criminals acting as terrorists, insane terrorists, and organizational terrorists. Each of these merits a brief examination.

Political terrorists and religious fanatics are among the oldest types of terrorists. Convinced that their views are correct, they use terrorism as their sole or primary weapon in their efforts to achieve their purposes. Political terrorists generally seek to radically change the "whole system." Recently, most political terrorists have been Marxists who generally have specific demands to make and who believe that American companies are the root of all evil. A variant of this type, religious fanatics, will readily give their lives because they feel God will reward them for killing His enemies. An individual committed to being a martyr may not articulate any demands. It has even been suggested that the term "fundamentalist" and to a lesser extent "orthodox" almost imply individuals and/or organizations that are or could easily resort to terrorism. One example of this type of terrorist is those engaged in the New York World Trade Center bombing.

Average citizen turned terrorist is a type related to political terrorists. These are ordinary citizens who turn terrorists, frequently members of environmental, anti-nuclear, animal rights, anti-abortion, anti-government, or religious groups who have come to feel that "working within the system" is unsatisfactory, so the only recourse is violence. The average citizen turned terrorist generally is seeking not to "overthrow the system" but rather to change only one particular part of it. The most notable recent example of terrorism carried out by American citizens was the Oklahoma City bombing.

Criminals acting as terrorists, while sometimes propounding political views, create fear and intimidation through their terrorist acts for the purpose of obtaining large sums of money quickly. In other words, these are criminals who use political excuses to mask their real motivations. Many cases of international kidnapping are carried out by this type of terrorist. In the United States, criminal-bandit terrorism has been largely confined to what we call organized crime and, to a lesser extent, organized gangs. More recently, however, other copycat criminals appear to be emerging.

Insane terrorists are individuals suffering from psychological disorders and are frequently "copycats" desiring attention more than making a point or seeking money. Acting irrationally, they use violent tactics such as shooting, bombing, or kidnapping; and their goals may be only remotely or strangely related to the targets they choose (or to the people who become the inadvertent victims). In many ways, this is the most difficult type of terrorism to prevent since there is virtually no way to predict what mentally disturbed individuals are likely to do. One of the most recent and best-known examples of a mentally unstable terrorist is the Unabomber.

Organizational terrorists are members, former members, or other constituents of an organization who use gossip, political tactics, harassment, intimidation, and threats to create a climate of fear that will enable them to further their own objectives. They prey upon the fears of managers trying to cope with the unknown and a maze of legal constraints. Most often, organizational terrorists are intelligent and creative individuals who understand the line between behavior that is legally permissible and that which is not. They may try to get others to speak up while they remain quietly behind the scenes, thus minimizing their risk. Organizational terrorists mask their real goals by hiding behind a legitimate issue that they anticipate the group will support. They may use anonymous letters, notes, and/or memos to lend credence to their ideas or to discredit others. In like manner, they may simply spread malicious gossip to discredit ideas or people. In any event, their goal is personal gain and their tactic is to terrorize—create a climate of fear—the organization in a relatively low-key manner, without bringing undue legal attention upon themselves.

One example of an organizational terrorist is an employee who threatens legal action when his or her unjustified requests are turned down, whether they be relatively simple requests (e.g., a modification of policies, a change in procedure, time off for personal business), or larger demands such as a change in assignment, a promotion, or a salary increase that would most likely constitute favoritism or reverse discrimination. Similarly, an individual who possesses vital information or company secrets which, if divulged, would significantly harm the company may attempt to use that knowledge for personal purposes and, hence, become an organizational terrorist. Organizational terrorists may also be employees in powerful positions within the organization or "bullies" who are accustomed to using such tactics in all of their interpersonal interactions.

Another example of an organizational terrorist is an individual who attempts to discredit someone or some organization by intentionally spreading false or misleading information. The use of slander and misinformation campaigns, especially through the use of computers, is increasing. For example, a disgruntled employee or customer may attempt to discredit a company in the eyes of customers so they will not buy the company's product or service. If the objective is to create fear in the customers, the act is clearly terrorism; if not, it is "only" yet another form of workplace violence, sabotage, or dysfunctional behavior in organizations. Examples of this could include Internet revenge.

Why They Do It

Terrorism is designed to get attention. While the motivation is supposedly ideological, oftentimes, the real reason is financial. Their methods are ruthless, and their victims may not even be connected with their targets. Religious fanatics, in particular, select targets to inflict maximum pain and damage. Criminal terrorists want money, so business represents their primary targets. Insane terrorists are unpredictable but may attack a businessperson to try to enact revenge on a business that they feel has wronged them in some way. The citizen turned terrorist generally feels that the "system" is not working for them or is even working against them so that they cannot settle differences peacefully and, hence, they turn to violence in their anger. Anti-nuclear groups break into military facilities to destroy military equipment; anti-abortionists blow up clinics and shoot doctors; animal rights advocates criminally trespass research labs and destroy experiments or free animals.

Terrorism also impacts organizations. Most Americans kidnapped overseas are businesspeople who are held for ransom. Ransom is very costly. $60 million was paid by an Argentina firm; Firestone paid $3 million in Argentina; Exxon, $14.2 million in Argentina; Goodyear, $10 million in Guatemala; and Amoco, $3 million in Argentina. Bombings cost businesses at least $88 million in 1981 and over $100 million in 1982.

The costs, of course, are not always easily expressed in dollar terms. Morale and productivity impacts can occur that are not readily measured. Terrorists may attack only where it hurts most; e.g., computers. The harassment of workers by terrorists causes employees to "lose confidence in the company's ability to protect them." The resulting stress not only reduces productivity but also affects the family outside of work, destroying peoples' social life; it's hard to concentrate on your job when you are worried about your life or your family.

What Can Organizations Do About It?

Organizations need to respond to terrorism in advance. It has been reported that of the Fortune 1000 companies 88 percent have building security checks, 66 percent employ burglar alarms, 48 percent use closed-circuit TV, 38 percent have electronic card ID systems, and 24 percent employ armed guards. Executive protection against kidnapping is fairly new but growing, particularly for overseas assignments.

Physical Setting

The physical plant should be refurbished to ensure that it is as secure as possible. All areas, both inside and out, should be well-lit with no shadow areas in which someone can hide. Coupled with the lights, landscaping should be arranged so that no one could hide behind shrubs or trees near walkways, parking lots, and buildings. Closed-circuit television should monitor interior corridors and stairwells as well as outside walkways and parking lots. Locks and sensors need to be controlled carefully to ensure limited access. To the extent possible, parking should be away from buildings and barriers (concrete benches, sculpture, trees) should be erected to prevent vehicles from getting near enough to buildings to be used as bomb locations.

Social/Psychological

Training. Everyone in the organization should receive training in defensive strategies and coping with emergencies.

Communication. A key element in any terrorist situation is communication. People need to be kept informed. Use as many forms of communication as possible and ensure that all communication is two-way. Answer questions quickly and honestly. As events unfold, issue frequent communications with everyone in the organization.

Employee Assistance Programs. Establish an employee assistance program (EAP). EAPs have come into existence to deal with substance abuse, rising health and safety costs, and increased stress in the workplace. EAP services may range from counseling to offering a wide range of employee services, including emergency financial aid assistance, wellness programs, legal aid services, carpool assistance, health and wellness equipment and workout gyms, smoking cessation assistance, and substance-abuse programs. Typically, EAPs have four objectives: assisting managers with performance deficits associated with personal problems; offering professional help to employees and their families; third educating employees to prevent future problems; and reducing the social stigma often associated with personal problems.

Thousands of organizations have EAPs so that is one piece of information that you will want to find out about any organization to which you apply for a job. Since 80 to 90 percent of all industrial accidents have been attributed to personnel problems, EAPs focused on prevention, treatment, and rehabilitation could save an organization a great deal of money. Indeed, the U.S. Bureau of Labor Statistics has estimated that $800 million invested in EAPs each year generates about $4 billion in total savings, and yet EAPs have been estimated to cost only $22 to $25 per employee per year.

Many EAPs are handled by external vendors or consultants to alleviate problems of confidentiality. Round-the-clock accessibility, availability of professional expertise, and geographic location also are factors contributing to the success or failure of the programs. Programs developed to deal with employee productivity and substance abuse seem to be regarded as valuable. Most employees were said to be helped by early detection and intervention. Once an employee problem was suspected, observation, documentation, confrontation, referral, and follow-up were needed.

Functions of an EAP after a terrorist incident normally would be to identify symptoms of employee stress, emotional problems, and substance abuse. Ways to reduce stress caused by terrorism could include management development programs to address problematic teamwork, personality types, decision-making skills, and sociopsychological interaction skills. Everyone may need some form of counseling or support group to cope with the trauma brought about by terrorism. Specialized trauma counselors should be brought in to assist with psychological debriefing for personnel. For those who want to be transferred, relocated, or retired, career assessment and development skills would be appropriate. Safety improvement and reduction of ergonomic factors that contribute to an employee's psychological and physical stress would also be covered.

Performance Decrements. Management must recognize that performance will be subnormal for a period of time. Fatigue, hurt, fear, and anger will initially distract everyone from their jobs. Absenteeism, tardiness, and general productivity declines are likely to continue for a while. Managerial personnel need to be aware of this and not complicate the problem by striving to return to normal performance levels too quickly.

The Crisis Plan

Every organization should have a crisis plan ready for immediate implementation as needed. An organizational crisis plan should have numerous elements. Everyone should have a list of telephone numbers and addresses of those with whom they are associated at work in case contact needs to be made. In the event of an emergency, locations where people will report to and actually perform their work should be identified. Likewise, in the event of an emergency, pay and benefit policies that are in force should be clearly understood. A variety of communication media should be established and utilized. An employee assistance program (EAP) should be established to help people cope with trauma. After an emergency, it is important to get key people back into facilities to assure others that it is safe (obviously the structural integrity of the facility must be first assured).

The Rewards for Justice Program

The U.S. Department of State offers rewards for information that could prevent acts of terrorism against United States persons or property or that could lead to the arrest or conviction of terrorists responsible for such acts. Rewards can be as high as $4 million when U.S. civil aviation is involved. The Rewards for Justice Program was created through the 1984 Act to Combat International Terrorism (Public Law 98-533). Under this program, cooperating individuals and their immediate family members may be relocated to the United States, or elsewhere, and they are assured complete confidentiality. Rewards, totaling millions of dollars, have been paid in more than 20 cases including the Operation Desert Storm case noted earlier.

At first, the emphasis in the program was on information that led to the arrest or conviction of those responsible for specific terrorist attacks. In 1988, however, the emphasis shifted to prevention. Then, six years after its establishment, the U.S. State Department formed a partnership with the Air Transport Association of America and the Air Line Pilots Association, International, in which each organization pledged up to $1 million to supplement rewards paid by the U.S. Government for information that prevents a terrorist act against U.S. civil aviation, or leads to the arrest and conviction of any person who has committed such an act. For cases not covered by the partnership agreement, the U.S. Government offers up to $2 million in rewards. A committee composed of representatives from the White House National Security Council staff, the Central Intelligence Agency, the Department of Justice, the Federal Bureau of

Investigation, the Drug Enforcement Administration, the U.S. Marshals Service Witness Security Program, the Immigration and Naturalization Service, the Federal Aviation Administration, the Department of Energy, and the Department of State recommends who gets the rewards and how much they are to get.

The State Department promotes the Rewards for Justice Program through publicity efforts to obtain public information about terrorist activity. Advertisements are designed to promote awareness of the Program and to reach those with information. Those ads appear in numerous languages in a wide variety of publication outlets. Additionally, public service announcements featuring entertainment personalities have appeared on radio.

Information to Seek

Clearly, you want as much information as you can get about any terrorist incidents or threats at any organization for which you are applying for a job. Some of the questions you may wish to seek answers to are the following (some overlap with previous chapters):

- Has this organization ever been the target of a terrorist act?
- Has this organization ever been the target of a terrorist threat?
- Does this organization have a crisis plan?
- Does this organization have an employee assistance program?
- Do you expect the main responsibilities for this position to change in the next six months to a year?
- What are the performance expectations of this position over the first 12 months?
- What are the company's most important values?
- What's different about working here than anywhere else you've worked?
- How has the company changed since you joined?
- How has the organization overcome challenges with remote work?
- Has this organization ever been the target of a terrorist act?
- Has this organization ever been the target of a terrorist threat?

- Does this organization have a crisis plan?
- Does this organization have an employee assistance program?

Chapter Takeaways

- Terrorism is happening.
- Five types of terrorists—political terrorists and religious fanatics, average citizen turned terrorist, criminals acting as terrorists, insane terrorists, and organizational terrorists.
- Terrorism is designed to get attention.
- Organizations can take actions to reduce issues—such as having an employee assistance program.
- The Rewards for Justice Program was started by the U.S. Department of State.

Think About This Chapter Again

Look over the notes you took before reading this chapter. What changes would you make now?

Think about this anecdote in relation to this chapter.

"I don't have a degree or certification. I learned everything at home, by doing. I was not accepted into a computer class in high school because my grades were okay (and I'm being nice here). Then I had to join the army (mandatory service) and was not accepted in to [sic] programming course, because I was in an Electronics class and not a Computer Science class in high school (well, again, wasn't accepted). I felt frustrated.

Today I'm 21, and after fighting hard to get into positions in the past, I find my latest year more efficient in terms of learning than any other period before (and I've been programming since 16, as a hobby). I was given chances and used the momentum wisely to learn and enhance my professional knowledge.

I started a job search three weeks ago. I sent my resume to five companies, and eventually passed all recruitment stages and got offers from all of them. That makes me proud because I was competing with graduates and people that are quite experienced.

Today, I was sponsored by my company and I possess the Highly Skilled Migrant status in a beautiful country. Working and living in a nice city, earning a very competitive salary, and getting nice benefits for doing what I love. Hard work pays out, eventually."

Source: Adopted from www.quora.com/What-is-your-success-story-to-get-a-job

Recommended Reading

The following could expand your understanding of the chapter's material:

Ackerman, G. A., and M. Burnham. 2021. "Towards a Definition of Terrorist Ideology." *Terrorism and Political Violence* 33 (6): 1160–1190.

Bakker, E. 2015. *Terrorism and Counterterrorism Studies: Comparing Theory and Practice.* Leiden University Press.

Howie, L. 2007. "The Terrorism Threat and Managing Workplaces." *Disaster Prevention and Management* 16 (1): 70–78.

Van Fleet, D. D., and E. W. Van Fleet. 2006. "Internal Terrorists: The Terrorists Inside Organizations." *Journal of Managerial Psychology* 21 (8): 763–774.

CHAPTER 8

Psychological Safety

Make some notes of what you expect in this chapter. Write down what you feel are the main points. Keep that in mind as you read this chapter.

Thus far, only physical safety has been discussed, but physical safety and security are only part of the picture. Equally or possibly more important is psychological safety. Organizations ensure the safety and security of personnel and equipment, including protection from violence including, if possible, identifying and eliminating hazards and security risks.[1] "Psychological safety is created by leaders who have the humility and courage to seek ideas and insights from the employees they serve. This is how to create a learning culture and encourage followers to become their best."[2]

A truly safe environment tends to be one that ensures physical safety and security but also has management and the organization acting in such a way that helps people feel purposeful, motivated, and energized to achieve their best performance at work.[3] Psychological safety adds to a safer physical workplace by, among other ways, encouraging organization members to report potential hazards and safety issues. Organizations should provide working conditions that are tolerable as well as safe[4] and where there is psychological safety. Psychological safety exists when "people feel free and safe to ask questions, dare to speak their minds, are empowered to address and refute one another, where they report mistakes and talk about them, and express concerns or propose new ideas without being asked."[5]

To make sure that there is a connection between a physically safe workplace and a psychologically safe one, management and organizations should:

1. Support a psychologically safe workplace culture,
2. Encourage open communication,
3. Foster a learning mindset,

4. Be clear about expectations,

5. Support mental health and a recovery-ready workplace, and

6. Be supportive (https://www.nsc.org/workplace/safety-topics/
   psychological-safety-correlates-to-physical-safety).

*Are you bored with life? Then throw yourself into some work you be-
lieve in with all your heart, live for it, die for it, and you will find
happiness that you had thought could never be yours.*

—*Dale Carnegie*

There are various ways to develop psychological safety in an organization. Among them are Four Stages, Five Pillars, and the Playbook. You
should refer to the references for these to learn more about the particular
approach but highlights are presented here.[6]

Four Stages

Psychological safety occurs when all four stages exist. The four stages refer
to conditions in which those in the organization feel (1) included, (2) safe
to learn, (3) safe to contribute, and (4) safe to challenge the status quo.[7]
"To create a truly inclusive and psychologically safe environment, organizations must integrate and prioritize all four stages. Each stage builds
upon the previous one, creating a progression that nurtures a culture of
psychological safety from its foundation. By recognizing the intercon-
nectedness of these stages, organizations can ensure that psychological
safety becomes an integral part of their values, practices, and norms."[8]

Five Pillars

The Five Pillars approach is implemented through training programs by
Gina Battye.[9] The pillars are (1) self—bring your whole self to work, (2)
social—build social capital in the workplace, (3) collaboration—cultivate
powerful and successful collaboration, (4) curiosity—experiment and
question to innovate, and (5) creativity—generate solutions to transcend
boundaries. Integrating the five pillars leads to psychological safety.

The Psychological Safety Playbook

A unique approach to developing psychological safety in an organization uses plays or vignettes to stimulate the reader's thinking.[10] These are presented in a little book (Helbig and Norman, 2023), the size of which should not diminish its impact. The book presents five short plays. The five plays are: (1) communicate courageously, (2) master the art of listening, (3) manage your reactions, (4) embrace risk and failure, and (5) design inclusive rituals. Each play begins with a short vignette followed by five "moves" or issues designed to cause the reader to examine his or her reactions to the play and the point being made. The plays and moves are:

- Communicate Courageously
  - Welcoming other viewpoints, soliciting diverse perspectives, expressing your own emotions, taking off the mask of perfection, and nurturing a sense of humor at work.
- Master the Art of Listening
  - Listen to understand, be fully present, clarify your understanding, listen for emotions, and commit to curiosity.
- Manage Your Reactions
  - Model nondefensive reactions, respond productively, watch out for your blind spots, appreciate being challenged, and build on others' ideas.
- Embrace Risk and Failure
  - Normalize failure, reframe failures as learning opportunities, get comfortable with discomfort, model learner behavior, and celebrate continuous learning.
- Design Inclusive Rituals
  - Upgrade meetings, respect all voices, take turns, check for psychological safety, and appreciate the team.

The authors suggest that you experiment with the Playbook in group discussions and individually. More discussion helps to foster a climate of psychological safety.

V-REEL®

- In addition to these approaches to psychological safety, I suggest the use of the V-REEL® framework.[11] The framework was developed by Dr. David Flint[12] as a guide to assist organizations in creating value in their environment. It has been modified as an approach for developing psychological safety in organizations. The V-REEL letters as used here should be interpreted as follows:[13]
  - **V** indicates the value of having a psychologically and physically safe workplace.
  - **R** indicates the rareness of that value.
  - **E** the first E indicates factors, forces, conditions, policies, or behaviors that might erode (E) or chip away at your ability to create value.
  - **E** the second E indicates factors, forces, conditions, policies, or behaviors that enable (E) or help to create that value.
  - **L** indicates how long you have to obtain the value before it is too late, and how long you might expect the value to last.

Further Steps

In addition to these approaches, there are other steps that you should take to achieve psychological safety. Some of these overlap with the approach you may have taken. Those steps include the following.

- Demonstrate engagement.
- Show understanding.
- Be inclusive in interpersonal settings.
- Be inclusive in interpersonal settings.
- Show confidence and conviction without appearing inflexible.

Caution

Can an organization have too much psychological safety? Short-term performance could suffer if too much time is used for innovation or for dealing with criticisms from organizational members[14] although open communication about these sorts of effects should offset them.[15] And some organizations with substantial external rules and regulations, such as sports organizations, will necessarily curtail psychological safety to some degree.[16] The important point to remember is that psychological safety is a learning process aimed at long-term organizational success and not a short-term fix for problems.

Chapter Takeaways

- Physical safety and security are only part of the picture.
- Equally or possibly more important is psychological safety.
- Psychological safety exists when "people feel free and safe to ask questions, dare to speak their minds, are empowered to address and refute one another, where they report mistakes and talk about them, and express concerns or propose new ideas without being asked.
- Approaches to obtaining psychological safety are Four Stages, Five Pillars, the Playbook, and the V-REEL® framework.
- Psychological safety is a learning process.

Think About This Chapter Again

Look over the notes you took before reading this chapter. What changes would you make now?

Think about this anecdote in relation to this chapter.

"De Luca was 30 when she decided her current path wasn't working. Forced to start at the bottom, a former Macy's store manager and retail and furniture buyer bravely and confidently took a job as an editorial assistant at *Glamour*, where she was determined to make an early impression. And, indeed, De Luca did just that.

To get the job at *Glamour*, De Luca put her past experience into a story. Because she explains, 'people had a hard time believing I wanted to start from scratch,' she leveraged her retail background as a fresh perspective she'd offer the new gig. Then, not wanting to be 'editorial assistant forever,' she got promoted twice in three years, constantly reminding herself of past successes whenever she began to doubt herself.

Another thing De Luca did along the way was stay stimulated. Boredom is inevitable, and you can either allow it to creep in, take over, and drive you crazy, or you can manage it. Every time she found herself starting to feel bored, she 'made people aware.' Subsequently, she'd be given more work and greater responsibilities (not to mention promotions!).

I asked her specifically about starting over and working with people a lot younger than her, and De Luca stressed the importance of learning.

It's this candid communication that De Luca has continually found worthwhile—it's also something she learned from her mother at an early age. 'If you don't ask, you don't get,' De Luca's mom would say, encouraging her daughter to always put herself in touch with others who may be of assistance in some way. 'The more people who know [what you're looking for]—the right people who know—can help you strategize, think through it.'

Which is, in fact, a perfect segue to De Luca's golden networking advice: 'It's important to put yourself in places where people will have an opportunity to get to know you and what you stand for.' What you'll find is that 'there's always somebody to help you along the way.'

And that's pretty much how Vanessa De Luca rose to her success as editor-in-chief of a major women's magazine that's been around for nearly 50 years and has a circulation well over a million. She (I'd say simply, but the ambition and dedication she dedicated along the way would refute that description) worked her way up, and up—and up— always throwing her hat in the ring when opportunities presented themselves and never allowing herself to get stuck.

Making a decision to change careers—regardless of how old you are—isn't easy, not on top of your day job. But it can be done. 'If your mind is set on it,' De Luca notes, you'll make it happen. In many ways, just knowing you're ready for something new means your course is already in motion."

Source: Adopted from www.themuse.com/advice/this-career-changer-proves-its -never-too-late-to-start-back-at-the-bottom

Recommended Reading

The following could expand your understanding of the chapter's material:

Battye, G. n.d. "The 5 Pillars of Psychological Safety." https://www.ginabattye.com/5-pillars-psychological-safety/.

Clark, T. R. 2020. *The 4 Stages of Psychological Safety*. Berrett-Koehler Publishers, Inc.

Edmondson, A. C. 2019. *The Fearless Organization*. John Wiley and Sons.

Flint, D. 2018. *Think Beyond Value—Building Strategy to Win*. Morgan James Publishing.

Helbig, K., and M. Norman. 2023. *Psychological Safety Playbook*. Page Two Press.

Rigby, A. n.d. "Psychological safety at work: Why your team really needs it." https://getmarlee.com/blog/psychological-safety.

CHAPTER 9

Recent Developments

Make some notes of what you expect in this chapter. Write down what you feel are the main points. Keep that in mind as you read this chapter.
"You never know what's around the corner. It could be everything. Or it could be nothing. You keep putting one foot in front of the other, and then one day you look back and you've climbed a mountain."
—Tom Hiddleston

Recent developments have both eliminated and created jobs in rather significant ways. To assure that your job search is successful, an understanding of those developments should be quite useful.

Events

The COVID-19 pandemic resulted in major job losses. Termed "The Great Resignation," in 2022, it led to 50 million workers quitting their jobs, although in 2023, things were a bit better.[1] The U.S. job market was more stable in 2024, but then early in 2025, it turned for the worse largely because the U.S. president caused layoffs in the government that led to repel effects in the private sector.[2]

The executive coaching firm of Challenger, Gray, and Christmas Incorporated indicated that in January and February of 2025, over 200,000 jobs were lost. This was more than the same period in 2024.[3] The U.S. Bureau of Labor Statistics reported that the unemployment rate was around 4 percent, with employment trending up in health care, financial activities, transportation and warehousing, and social assistance, while Federal government employment declined.[4] Jobs are being cut in every sector, and they are expected to continue in 2025.[5] Technology, manufacturing, government, and health care have been the industries hit the hardest.[6]

It is expected that rapid changes will occur that are likely to stunt employment growth, eliminating some roles that took off during tech's rise. However, there is room for optimism. Low-paying work, such as home health or personal care aides, will grow, as will that of other health care professions like nurse practitioners, physician assistants, and health service managers.[7] Technology, clean energy, Information security analysts, data science, statisticians, solar photovoltaic installers, and wind turbine service technicians are also expected to see increases in jobs.[8]

Your success in finding a job still hinges on core principles—authenticity, persistence, and patience. (1) Authenticity—Tailor your message to the company but stay true to yourself. (2) Persistence—Rejection is inevitable in a competitive landscape, but those who learn, adapt, and stay the course will find success. Here's how to stay persistent without burning out: Set Small Goals, Follow Up Thoughtfully, Learn and Adapt. (3) Patience—This is an essential survival skill in 2025. The process can be slow: a recruiter reviews your resume, you attend multiple interviews, and then—finally—an offer. Or maybe not.[9]

Types

An executive from Manpower indicated that 65 percent of workers in the future will have jobs that don't even exist today. He further argues that automation will change the workplace, but it will both eliminate and create different kinds of jobs.[10] New-Collar and B-Corp jobs are available for first-time job seekers. Encore jobs are for those interested in a second career.

New-Collar Jobs

An emerging trend reshaping the workforce is the rise of new-collar jobs. New-collar jobs emphasize technical skills and practical expertise over formal education. Types of new-collar jobs include Cybersecurity Analyst, Data Analyst, Medical Coding Specialist, Cloud Computing Specialist, HVAC Technician, IT Support Specialist, Digital Marketing Specialist, Electrician, Web Developer, Robotics Technician, Pharmacy Technician, UX Designer, Wind Turbine Technician, Video Game Tester, and Solar Panel Installer.[11]

Know that it takes training and time to obtain a new-collar job. Focus your attention on gaining a better understanding of opportunities available to you and that are of interest to you. New-collar jobs require some special skills and training, but you may already have them. Factor in your passions and interests as you consider possible jobs and careers. If you feel a more flexible schedule would work to your benefit, consider online options for training.[12]

B-Corp Jobs

Join a B-Corp company and be as passionate about making a difference. B-Corp businesses set high standards of social and environmental performance, accountability, and transparency.[13] Companies that are certified as B-Corp are Patagonia, Ben & Jerry's, Tech Superpowers, Seventh Generation, New Belgium Brewing, Allbirds, Sunrise Banks, Warby Parker, King Arthur Baking Company, Danone North America, Bronner's, Bombas, Kickstarter, Eileen Fisher, The Steadman Group, AllCare Health, Aspiration, Geek Girl Tech, New Leaf Paper, and Aveda.

To find a job in a B-Corp, use B-Work. It regularly adds new job openings from Certified B Corporations. You may also find LinkedIn, B Lab Global, and Mac's List to be helpful. And, of course, networking plays an influential role.[14]

Encore Jobs

Encore jobs are second-career jobs that occur later in a person's life. They frequently combine income and greater personal meaning or social impact.[15] Many encored jobs are available in not-for-profit organizations, particularly in fundraising, marketing, and program management.[16] There are also opportunities in education, health care, renewable energy, sustainable agriculture, and green building.[17]

Chapter Takeaways

- Recent developments have upset the job market, but there is room for optimism.
- There is a rise in New-Collar and B-Corp jobs.
- Second-career opportunities exist in encore jobs.

Think About This Chapter Again

Look over the notes you took before reading this chapter. What changes would you make now?

Think about these anecdotes in relation to this chapter.

The Foundation of Your Success

Imagine walking into an interview with your head held high, completely confident in who you are and what you bring to the table. That's the power of a strong self-story. Right now, many job seekers are battling impostor syndrome and negative self-talk that's holding them back. But not you.

Your self-story isn't about fabricating achievements or putting on a fake persona. It's about honestly and positively reframing your experiences, skills, and potential. It's time to ditch the self-doubt and start believing in yourself. When you can articulate your value with genuine confidence, hiring managers will take notice.[18]

"I went on one interview that was at a business professional-type place, and everything seemed to be going well. Three interviews in, everything was still smooth, when the old woman asked if I had any tattoos or piercings. I thought that was pretty personal, and while I was vague with my answers, I told her that yes, I had some piercings done, but took them out. She actually stood up, asked me to stand up, and got right into my face. I did have some scarring from a lip ring and several nose rings, and she was looking at me so mean at that point that I told her I felt uncomfortable. She said, 'Well, with the scars, we won't hire you.' OK, BYE! I got a job a week later anyway, but damn ... that was really weird. And that company ended up shutting down 5 years later, so screw 'em." —witchyribbon84[19]

Recommended Reading

The following could expand your understanding of the chapter's material:

Deasy, M. 2025. "B Corp Jobs: 7 Top Tips to Land Your Ideal Impactful Career." https://www.impctdrvn.com/blog/b-corp-jobs-7-top-tips.

Mascali, M. n.d. "Your Guide to New-Collar Jobs." https://www.monster.com/career-advice/article/new-collar-jobs-1216.

Tolbert, T. 2025. "Navigating the 2025 Job Market: Challenges, Frustrations, and New Opportunities." https://www.linkedin.com/pulse/navigating-2025-job-market-challenges-frustrations-new-tasha-tolbert-0rwne/.

CHAPTER 10

Final Words

Make some notes of what you expect in this chapter. Write down what you feel are the main points. Keep that in mind as you read this chapter.

Your choice of a career is important, but careers can and do change. Do a self-assessment. One piece of advice is to keep learning. Stay in school or go back to school; take advantage of training programs from your current organization or local organizations; keep developing your skills and broadening your qualifications. Understand the fit between you and your career and recognize that there are four career stages: exploration, establishment, maintenance, and decline. Which stage are you currently in?

Try to learn as much as you can about the job and the organization and the people involved. Getting as much information as you can ahead of time and asking questions of people in the organization are vital to any successful job search. Try to find out ahead of time all you can about the organization, its people, and the job. To begin, check the organization's website. Also, search online for negative information about the organization, but be aware that (a) what you see may be distorted and (b) finding nothing is not a guarantee that there is nothing negative about the organization—it just means that nothing has been posted yet. Everyone tends to put on their "best faces" during job searches so that "what you see" is not necessarily "what you will get." If you don't like what you see, don't pursue the job any further unless you absolutely have no other alternatives.

If opportunity doesn't knock, then build a door.

—Milton Berle

Now, it's time to focus on the interview. As you prepare, here are some questions you may wish to ask:

General:

- May I have a detailed description of the skills, experience, and traits needed for this job?
- Describe a typical day for someone on this job.
- What are you looking for in a successful candidate?
- What do you see as my strengths and shortcomings in this position?
- In your view, how does my background fit with your requirements for his position?
- Why is this position open?
- How often has this position been filled in the past 5 to 10 years, and where have those people gone?
- When was the last time someone left this job, and why did that person leave? And the person before that?
- What kind of equipment is used on the job? What is the worst thing about this job?
- What is expected in terms of day-to-day performance on this job? What significant changes do you foresee in the future?
- What is the compensation for this job (don't accept "competitive" or "based on experience," and don't expect an exact number but rather a salary range)?

Organizational Culture/Climate:

- Describe the organization's culture and values
- What is the safety and health policy?
- Is there an EAP—employee assistance program?
- Is there tuition reimbursement or other support for training and education?
- Are there organizational training programs for employees?
- What will I have a chance to learn?
- What is your perception of the job and department?
- When did you start here and why do you stay?
- How is this job seen within the department and the department within the organization?
- Is there a complaint or grievance system?

Bosses, Coworkers, and Clients:

- With whom will I work and what are their backgrounds?
- How long do workers usually stay in their jobs here?

- Is there a current organization chart available?
- Describe the management style of the supervisor for this job?
- Are there opportunities to provide feedback about supervisors and/or coworkers to management?

Rewards and Advancement Opportunities:

- How is performance on the job evaluated?
- What are some of the objectives that you would like accomplished in this job?
- What freedom would I have in determining my work objectives, deadlines, and methods of measurement?
- What is most pressing? What would you like to have done within the next two or three months?
- What are some of the long-term objectives you would like completed?
- What are the key milestones you expect me to reach and within what period of time?
- What are some of the more difficult problems one would face in this position? How do you think these could be handled best?
- What are the benefits, advancement or rotational policies and work arrangements (e.g., flexible schedules, compensatory time, or telecommuting)?
- A year from now, if I do an excellent job for you, what type of increase can I expect? How does this differ from the average?
- Where could a person advance if successful in this position? Within what time frame?
- In what ways were you most pleased with the performance of the last person who held this position?
- Where is the greatest room for improvement?
- What would you like done differently by the next person who fills the job?

Summary Questions:

- What are the questions that I did not ask you but should have?
- What is the next step in this process? When can I expect to hear from you?
- When may I call you to follow up?

As the interview concludes, thank the interviewer. Afterward, send a short letter of thanks as well. Following up after an interview is one more way in which you can get a sense of the organization's culture. How was your follow-up handled? Was it ignored, responded to in a very mechanistic way, or warmly dealt with? A failure to respond promptly is not necessarily a "no, thanks." Some organizations prefer not to be bothered with additional contacts, so they only respond when they issue a job offer. On the other hand, following up is important and can actually influence whether you get the job. Following up suggests that you are interested. It also suggests certain personal characteristics such as resolve, attention to detail, and the ability to follow through.

There are several ways to follow up. Telephone calls disrupt the receiver and take too much time. Written approaches are generally more professional. Using regular postal service or e-mail, you can send a simple card, note, or letter indicating that you appreciated the opportunity of an interview and look forward to hearing the decision in the near future. Usually, it is best to keep it brief. The important thing about following up is that you do it. Following up can make a difference in whether you get an offer, and it may also furnish you with important perceptions about what working for the organization would be like. Who knows, even if you don't get this job, maybe the organization will have another one in the future.

What's Next?

Not all problems that you could encounter have been covered in this book, but we hope that enough have been identified to arm you with useful information. This final chapter wraps this up and opens the way for you to begin your job search.

Chapter Takeaways

- Careers are important.
- Learn about the job and the organization and the people.
- Interview questions.
- Follow-up.

Think About This Chapter Again

Look over the notes you took before reading this chapter. What changes would you make now?

Think about this anecdote in relation to this chapter.

"One place almost killed me.

It was a full-day interview, and I thought it had gone pretty well. I wasn't sure it was the place for me just due to the vibe, but I didn't feel like I'd failed or anything. It went crazy on the ride home.

The person who was driving me to the airport had picked up a Zipcar-like thing from Enterprise. She immediately apologized because 'The emergency brake is on, but I can't figure out how to release it.' I looked and said that it was one of the pedal ones, and she needed to push down on it with her foot to release it. So she did, and off we went.

As we drove, I noticed that she was driving a little erratically. We kept hitting the ridges on the right and then she would correct. Since the driver was correcting, I tried to remain calm because I knew the airport wasn't far. Also, it was still a job interview, and I didn't want to be critical.

Then she didn't correct. We hit the ridges, and I hoped she'd correct, but she didn't. I said, 'Um ... [Name],' but it was too late, and we slammed into the guard rails (we were on a bridge). That woke her up! She apologized, and we made it to the airport a few minutes later. My door was smashed so badly, I had to crawl out the driver's side door.

I wasn't hurt, luckily. As it turned out, the rubber had come off the emergency brake pedal. When it released, it cut her foot, and she was driving erratically because she was lightheaded and trying not to pass out. She did not drive home after dropping me off.

I didn't get the job. I apparently came in second. Which was OK—I don't know if I would have fit in well there. Funny thing though: A friend of mine got an interview with the same place later. He told me that they were having a driver pick him up instead of a member of the search committee, and he thought that was weird.

I knew why!"

Source: Adopted from https://www.themuse.com/advice/7-crazy-interview-stories-you-wont-believe-are-true

---

Recommended Reading

The following could expand your understanding of the chapter's material:

Van Fleet, D. D. 2024. *Dysfunctional Organizations*. Business Expert Press..

Van Fleet, D. D. 2025. *The Manager's Guide to Psychological Safety*. Business Expert Press.

Van Fleet, E. W., and D. D. Van Fleet. 2007. *Workplace Survival: Dealing with Bad Bosses, Bad Workers, Bad Jobs*. Publish America.

Appendixes

Appendix A

Learning More About Workplace Violence

American Society for Industrial Security
1655 North Fort Myer Dr.
Arlington, VA 22209
Telephone: (703)522-5800

American Psychological Association
750 First Street, NE
Washington, D.C., 20006

U.S. Centers for Disease Control and Prevention
1600 Clifton Road, NE
Atlanta, GA 30333

Crime Victims Research and Treatment Center
Medical University of South Carolina
151 Ashley Ave.
Charleston, SC 29425
Telephone: (803)792-2945

Crisis Management International, Inc.
Eight Piedmont Center, Suite 420
Atlanta, GA 30305
Telephone: 404-841-3400

National Crime Prevention Council
1700 K Street, NW, Suite 618
Washington, D.C., 20006
Telephone: (202)466-6272

National Crisis Prevention Institute, Inc.
3315 K, North 124th Street
Brookfield, WI 53005
Telephone: 800-558-8976

National Institute for Mental Health
5600 Fishers Lane
Rockville, MD 20857
Telephone: (301)496-4000

National Safe Workplace Institute
3008 Bishops Ridge
Monroe, NC 28110
Telephone: 704-289-6061

National Trauma Services
3554 Front Street
San Diego, CA 92103
Telephone: 800-398-2811

NIOSH—Atlanta
1600 Clifton Road, NE
Atlanta, CA 30333
Telephone: (404)639-3061

NIOSH Educational Resource Center—California
Center for Occupational and Environmental Health
Richmond Field Station
1301 S. 46th Street, Building 102
Richmond, CA 94804
Telephone: (510)231-5645

NIOSH
4676 Columbia Parkway
Cincinnati, OH 45226-1998
Telephone 1-800-35-NIOSH
Fax: (513)533-8573

Occupational Safety and Health Administration
1120 20th St. NW
Washington, D.C., 20036
Telephone: (202)219-8148

OSHA Consultation Services—California
CAL/OSHA Consultation Service
Telephone: (415)703-4050

Physicians for a Violence-Free Society
P.O. Box 35528
Dallas, TX 75235-0528
Telephone: (214)590-8807

Post Trauma Resources
1830 Bull Street
Columbia, SC 2920
Telephone: (803)765-0700

Public Health Service
DHHS Region I Office
John F. Kennedy Federal Building
Government Center, Room 1875
Boston, MA 02203
Telephone: (617)565-1439

Public Health Service
DHHS Region IV Office
101 Marietta Tower, Suite 1106
Atlanta, GA 30323
Telephone: (404)331-2396

Public Health Service
DHHS Region VIII Office
1185 Federal Building
1961 Stout Street
Denver, CO 80294
Telephone: (303)844-6166

Scripps Center Quality Management
(Crisis Management Services)
9747 Business Park Ave.
San Diego, CA 92131
Telephone: (619)566-3472

Society of Human Resources Mgmt.
606 N. Washington Street
Alexandria, VA 22314
Telephone: (703)548-3440

United States Department of Labor
200 Constitution Ave. NW
Washington, D.C., 20210

Appendix B

Internet Sites of Interest About Violence

Federal Protective Service
https://www.dhs.gov/federal-protective-service

The Injury & Violence Prevention Network
https://www.safestates.org/page/IVPN

Law Enforcement Agencies on the Web
https://post.ca.gov/federal-law-enforcement-agencies

National Crisis Prevention Institute
https://www.crisisprevention.com/

NIOSH
https://www.cdc.gov/niosh/fedreg/index.html

OSHA
https://www.osha.com/courses/outreach.html?utm_source=google&
utm_medium=cpc&utm_campaign=13963998940&utm_
content=154151573400&utm_term=osha&gad_source=1&gad_
campaignid=13963998940&gbraid=0AAAAAD7gr3GpjAFEp_
mTWl1IvbHH9kFJX&gclid=Cj0KCQjwj8jDBhD1ARIsACRV2T
sMJSbo7qFs4E1WgyoeGGwKiM1ZCpynEtetghJ3nD6MHzb1t
76VK44aAkVAEALw_wcB

Pavnet (Partners Against Violence Network) Information
https://www.ojp.gov/ncjrs/virtual-library/abstracts/pavnet-partnerships-
against-violence-network#:~:text=The%20Partnerships%
20Against%20Violent%20Network,%2C%20technical%20
assistance%2C%20and%20funding

Satore Township
www.crl.com/%7Emikekell/

United States Department of Justice
www.usdoj.gov/

Violence at Work and School
https://www.dhs.gov/archive/school-and-workplace-violence

Appendix C

Learning More About Job Hunting

Beaty, R. H. 1996. *175 High Impact Resumes*. New York: John Wiley and Sons, Inc.

Bell, A. H. 1997. *Great Jobs Abroad*. New York: McGraw-Hill.

Boole, R. N. 1996. *The 1996 What Color Is Your Parachute?* Berkeley, CA: Ten Speed Press.

Dixon, P. 1998. *Job Searching Online for Dummies*. Foster City, CA: IDG Books Worldwide.

Edwards, P., and S. Edwards. 1996. *Finding Your Perfect Work*. New York: G. P. Putnam's Sons.

Eikelberry, C. 1995. *The Career Guide for Creative and Unconventional People*. Berkeley, CA: Ten Speed Press.

Fear, R. A., and R. J. Chiron. 1990. *The Evaluation Interview*. New York: McGraw-Hill.

Frank, W. S. 1993. *200 Letters for Job Hunters*. Berkeley, CA: Ten Speed Press.

Freedman, H. S. 1986. *How to Get a Headhunter to Call*. New York: John Wiley and Sons, Inc.

Greene, S. D., and M. C. L. Martel. 1998. *The Ultimate Job Hunter's Guidebook*. 2nd edition; Boston: Houghton Mifflin Company.

Hall, D. T. 1976. *Careers in Organizations*. Santa Monica, Calif.: Goodyear.

Hirsch, A. S. 1996. *Love Your Work and Success Will Follow*. New York: John Wiley and Sons, Inc.

Kennedy, J. L., and T. J. Morrow. 1995. *Electronic Job Search Revolution*. New York: John Wiley and Sons, Inc.

Kozmetsky, R., and G. Kozmetsky. 1981. *Making It Together: A Survival Manual for the Executive Family*. New York: Free Press.

Krannich, R. L., and C. R. Krannich. 1995. *The Best Jobs for the 1990s and into the Twenty-first Century*. Manassas Park, VA: Impact Publications.

Krantz, L. 1995. *Jobs Rated Almanac*. 3rd edition; New York: John Wiley and Sons, Inc.

Medley, H. A. 1993. *Sweaty Palms: The Neglected Art of Being Interviewed*. Berkeley, CA: Ten Speed Press.

Tiegeer, P. D., and B. Barron-Tieger. 1995. *Do What You Are*. Boston: Little, Brown and Company.

Tien, E., and V. Frankel. 1996. *The I Hate My Job Handbook*. New York: Fawcett Columbine.

Appendix D

Internet Sites of Interest About Job Hunting

4Work.com
www.4work.com/

Academe This Week
chronicle.merit.edu/.ads/.links.html

America's Job Bank
www.ajb.dni.us/

Best Jobs USA
www.bestjobsusa.com

Black Collegian
www.black-collegian.com

Career and Job Help
https://www.public.asu.edu/~vanfleet/career.htm

CareerBuilder
www.careerbuilder.com/

CareerCast
www.careercast.com/

CareerCity
www.careercity.com/

career.com
www.career.com/

CareerMart
www.careermart.com/

Career Mosaic
www.careermosaic.com

CareerPath.com
www.careerpath.com/

CareerWeb
www.cweb.com/

College Grad Job Hunter
www.collegegrad.com/

E.span
www.espan.com

JobBank USA
www.jobbankusa.com/

JobDirect
www.jobdirect.com/

JobTrak
www.jobtrak.com/

NationJob Network
www.nationjob.com/

Net-Temps
www.net-temps.com/

Online Career Center
www.occ.com/

The Internet Job Locator
www.joblocator.com/jobs/

The Monster Board
www.monster.com/

TOPJobs USA
www.topjobsusa.com/

Women's Wire
Womenswire.com/work/?wcicareer

Yahoo! Classifieds
classifieds.yahoo.com/employment.html

Appendix E

Job Search Checklist

Following a checklist to guide your actions during a job search is both helpful and strategic. Given the impact the COVID-19 pandemic has had on business and all processes related to interviewing and hiring, using this guide will be to keep your search on track.

Are You Ready?

I have examined my emotions related to the layoff and am feeling, or starting to feel, optimistic and excited to begin job searching. Everyone deals with transition differently. There are five stages of transition that you might find yourself experiencing: shock/denial, depression, panic, anger, and finally optimism. These emotions, while completely normal, may affect your job search success.

I understand that the job search process today has changed from the last time I looked for a job and I understand the impact the pandemic has had on the overall job search and interview processes. I am ready to incorporate new strategies into my search.

Discover Your Focus

I have identified my target(s) for my next role including job title, industry, location, and salary.

I have thoroughly researched and chosen at least 10 target companies in my area.

I have defined my story and prepared my professional branding documents, including my Professional Value Proposition (PVP), resume, and LinkedIn profile.

I understand how to effectively tailor my resume for the different roles for which I am applying.

Plan Your Approach, Organize Your Search

Build Opportunities:

I have built a pipeline of potential opportunities and will not let it get below 7 at any given time (e.g., a promising networking conversation, a scheduled interview, or a hot job lead from a referral).

I review my job leads regularly and I search for new job leads online, only applying to those that are a good match for my skills and background.

Networking:

I have familiarized myself with online video meeting tools and understand how to best present myself on video.

I have reached out to my friends, family, and acquaintances and let them know I am looking for a job and I am expanding my network with new contacts to help uncover job leads.

I have set up my LinkedIn profile, and I actively use LinkedIn for research and networking.

I have posted my resume on a few key job boards so companies can find me when they're looking.

I follow up with my networking contacts on a regular basis and I ask for introductions to others.

I am involved in a handful of professional and community groups; I attend their virtual events now and actively participate in conversations. When things open again, I will attend in-person events (www.meetup. com, local chamber of commerce, job fairs, etc.).

I have identified appealing volunteer organizations and do what I can to support them virtually now; I am ready to spend some time each week volunteering in person when possible. These actions will help me fill the gap in my resume (www.volunteermatch.org).

I have registered with a handful of staffing firms.

Plan Your Time:

My Job Search Organizer is up-to-date—I keep track of all my activities including networking meetings, follow-ups, interviews, job applications, and other interactions.

I spend 70 percent of my job search time each week focused on outreach and networking activities.

I research trends in my industry and am working on developing new skills to align with demands in the market.

I maintain a regular schedule of activities for each day of the week and use a calendar system to stay organized.

I do five things for my job search five days per week, each day having at least one virtual networking meeting.

I do something fun for myself each week, eat right, and exercise to keep a healthy balance in my life.

I celebrate my successes.

Execute Your Plan, Refine as Necessary, and Land Your Next Opportunity

Interview Like a Pro

I have practiced using video meeting tools for interviews, ensuring my background, lighting and appearance are appropriate for an interview.

I am confident in researching companies and interviewers and feel prepared for my interviews.

I have practiced my SMART Stories and have specific examples of past accomplishments to present during conversations.

I feel that I excel in all of my interviews.

I consistently follow up after all of my interviews.

Negotiate Your Best Possible Offer

I have researched my field of work, the industry and my market to understand salary and compensation levels for someone with my experience.

I thoroughly understand the compensation negotiation process and strategy.

I know what I need from a job offer for it to be acceptable, and what I am willing to compromise on.

I have received job offers.

Transition into Your Next Opportunity

I have accepted a new position.

I have updated my resume and LinkedIn profile with my new role.

I have informed and thanked all of my contacts and those who assisted me throughout my search.

I have set career development goals for continued networking and professional development.

Source: https://femmeforward.randstadrisesmart.com/static/media/JobSearchChecklist DuringPandemic.943616f285514d2b81e9.pdf

Notes

Chapter 1

1. *HBR Guide to Changing Your Career* (2018).
2. Bolles (1980).
3. Cole (1990).
4. Gilman and Blumenthal (1986).
5. Byrne and Cowan (1986).
6. Anonymous (2022); Benson and Thornton (1978); Duval and Courtney (1978).
7. O'Neill and O'Reilly (2010, 2011).
8. Flores (2025).
9. Unknown (1986).
10. Warner (2014).
11. Powell and Maniniero (1992).
12. Anthony (2024).
13. Unknown (1989).
14. Berlin (2024).
15. Kozmetsky and Kozmetsky (1981).
16. Van Fleet and Van Fleet (2014), chapter 12.
17. Yate (2006).

Chapter 2

1. Terrell (2020).
2. Rugaber (2014).
3. Agovino (2020).
4. Zielinski (2020).
5. Anonymous (n.d.).
6. Patrontasch (n.d.).
7. Anonymous (n.d.).
8. Van Fleet and Van Fleet (1998).
9. Van Fleet and Van Fleet (2006).

Chapter 3

1. Michaud (1995).
2. Vanta (2023); Patrontasch (n.d.).
3. Kuder (2017).
4. Hill and Trist (1953).
5. Nichols (1997).
6. Ibid.
7. Wang (1993).
8. Safety Leadership Conference (2025).
9. Alert Media (2022).
10. Haws (n.d.).

Chapter 4

1. Cleveland Clinic (2024); Landy et al. (1994).
2. Adam (2025).
3. Krantz and Lee (2015).
4. Ibid.
5. Ibid.
6. Unknown (1995).
7. U.S. Department of Labor (n.d.); Anonymous (n.d.); Kelly (1995).

Chapter 5

1. Savas (2019).
2. Kets de Vries and Rook (2018).
3. Van Fleet and Van Fleet (2014).

Chapter 6

1. National Institute for Occupational Safety and Health (2002).
2. Van Fleet, D. D. and Van Fleet, E. W. (2007); Van Fleet, E. W., and Van Fleet, D. D. (2007).
3. Based on Nater et al. (2023).
4. The Muse Editors (2024).

Chapter 7

1. This chapter is based on Van Fleet (2024).

Chapter 8

1. Duncan and Heighway (2014); Fuller (2019).
2. Edmondson (n.d.).
3. Cable (2018).
4. Bitsch and Olynk (2008); Bitsch et al. (2006).
5. Van Der Loo and Beks (2020).
6. See also Van Fleet (2025).
7. Clark and Ritter (2018); Clark (2020).
8. https://www.leaderfactor.com/
9. https://www.ginabattye.com/5-pillars-psychological-safety/
10. Helbig and Norman (2023).
11. Van Fleet (2024); Van Fleet (2025).
12. Flint (2018).
13. for details see Van Fleet (2024); Van Fleet (2025).
14. Carbajal (2024); Jansen (2021); Howatt (2024); Eldor et al. (2023); Eldor and Cappelli (2024); Weinstein (2023).
15. Maximo et al. (2019).
16. Taylor et al. (2022).

Chapter 9

1. Melhorn and Hoover (2025).
2. Valladares (2025).
3. Ibid.
4. Anonymous (2025).
5. Valladares (2025).
6. Tolbert (2025).
7. Schnitzer (2021).
8. Ibid.
9. The Marketing Recruiter (2025).
10. Staffing Industry Analysts (2017).
11. Mascali (n.d.).
12. This section based on Payscale (n.d.).
13. This section is based on Gentile (n.d.).
14. Deasy (2025).
15. Fuse Workforce Management (n.d).
16. WikiFreedom (n.d.).
17. Alboher (2012).
18. Work It Daily (2024).
19. Buzzfeed (2022).

Bibliography

Ackerman, G. A., and M. Burnham. 2021. "Towards a Definition of Terrorist Ideology." *Terrorism and Political Violence* 33 (6): 1160–1190.

Adam, J. 2025. "15 Low-Stress Jobs for 2025." https://money.usnews.com/careers/articles/low-stress-jobs.

Agovino, T. 2020. "Finding the Jobs of the Future." *HR Magazine* 65 (4): 74–77.

Alert Media. 2022. "3 Examples of Companies with Great Safety Culture." https://www.alertmedia.com/blog/safety-culture-examples/.

Aldwin, C. M. 2007. *Stress Coping and Development—An Integrative Perspective.* The Guilford Press.

Anonymous. (n.d.). "Managing Work-Related Stress." https://www.urmc.rochester.edu/encyclopedia/content?contenttypeid=1&contentid=2882.

Anonymous. 2025. "The Employment Situation—May 2025." Bureau of Labor Statistics. U.S. Department of Labor. https://www.bls.gov/news.release/pdf/empsit.pdf.

Bakker, E. 2015. *Terrorism and Counterterrorism Studies: Comparing Theory and Practice.* Leiden University Press.

Battye, G. n.d. "The 5 Pillars of Psychological Safety." https://www.ginabattye.com/5-pillars-psychological-safety/.

Belli, G. 2017. "65 Percent of Tomorrow's Workers Will Have Jobs That Don't Exist Today." https://www.payscale.com/career-advice/65-percent-tomorrows-workers-jobs-dont-exist-today/?opti_ca=22177837080&opti_ag=&opti_ad=&opti_key=&utm_medium=cpc&utm_

Benson, P. G., and G. C. Thornton III. 1978. "A Model Career Planning Program." *Personnel*, March–April, 30–39.

Berman, D. C. 1986. "Putting Employees Back on Track." *Bottomline* 3 (10): 19–22.

Bitsch, V., and N. J. Olynk. 2008. "Risk-Increasing and Risk-Reducing Practices in Human Resource Management: Focus Group Discussions with Livestock Managers." *Journal of Agricultural and Applied Economics* 40 (1): 185–201.

Bitsch, V., G. A. Kassa, S. B. Harsh, and A. W. Mugera. 2006. Human Resource Management Risks: Sources and Control Strategies Based on Dairy Farmer Focus Groups." *Journal of Agricultural and Applied Economics* 38 (01): 123–136.

Bolles, R. N. 1980. *What Color Is Your Parachute?* Ten Speed Press.

Bowen, D. D., and R. D. Hisrich. 1986. "The Female Entrepreneur: A Career Development Perspective," *Academy of Management Review* 11 (2): 393–407.

Bowman, S. 1994. *When the Eagle Screams*. Birch Lane Press Book/Carol Publishing Group.

Burnett, B., and D. Evans. 2016. *Designing Your Life: How to Build a Well-Lived, Joyful Life*. Alfred A. Knopf.

Buzzfeed. 2022. "Job-Hunting Is the Absolute Worst and These 20 Stories Prove It." https://www.buzzfeed.com/jessg/wildest-and-most-frustrating-job-interviews.

Byrne, J. A., and A. L. Cowan. 1986. "Should Companies Groom New Leaders or Buy Them?" *Business Week*, September 22, 94–96.

Cable, D. 2018. "How Humble Leadership Really Works." https://hbr.org/2018/04/how-humble-leadership-really-works.

Cannings, K., and C. Montmarquette. 1991. "Managerial Momentum: A Simultaneous Model of the Career Progress of Male and Female Managers." *Industrial and Labor Relations Review*, January 1, 212–228.

Carbajal, E. 2024. "Psychological Safety at Work Has Downsides, Studies Show." *Becker's Hospital Review*. https://www.beckershospitalreview.com/workforce/psychological-safety-at-work-has-downsides-studies-show.html.

Clark, C. M., and K. Ritter. 2018. Policy to Foster Civility and Support a Healthy Academic Work Environment." *Journal of Nursing Education* 57 (6): 325–331.

Clark, T. R. 2020. *The 4 Stages of Psychological Safety*. Berrett-Koehler Publishers, Inc.

Cleveland Clinic. 2024. "Stress." https://my.clevelandclinic.org/health/diseases/11874-stress.

Cole, D. 1990. "Assess Your Skills to Reduce Career Doubts." *The Wall Street Journal, The College Edition of the National Business Employment Weekly*, Spring, 7–8.

Conlon, P. 1987. "Show You Care." *Canadian Business*, Canada, 60(4).

Cook, M. F. 1991. "HR Crisis Management and Terrorist Threats," In *The Human Resources Yearbook: 1991 Edition*, edited by M. F. Cook. Prentice Hall.

Cooper, Cary, L., and P. Dewe. 2004. *Stress: A Brief History*, Blackwell Publishing.

Deasy, M. 2025. "B Corp Jobs: 7 Top Tips to Land Your Ideal Impactful Career." https://www.impctdrvn.com/blog/b-corp-jobs-7-top-tips.

Denenberg, R. V., and M. Braverman. 1999. *The Violence-Prone Workplace*. Cornell University Press.

Duffy, B. 1995. "The End of Innocence." *US News and World Report*, August 14, 34–50.

Duncan, M., and P. Heighway. 2014. *Health and Safety at Work Essentials*. 8th ed. Lawpack Publishing.

Duval, B. A., and R. S. Courtney. 1978. "Upward Mobility: The GF Way of Opening Employee Advancement Opportunities." *Personnel*, May–June, 43–53.

Edmondson, A. C. n.d. "Psychological Safety." https://amycedmondson.com/psychological-safety/.

Edmondson, A. C. 2019. *The Fearless Organization*. John Wiley and Sons.

Eldor, L., M. Hodor, and P. Cappelli. 2023. "The Limits of Psychological Safety: Nonlinear Relationships with Performance." *Organizational Behavior and Human Decision Processes* 177: 104255.

Eldor, L., and P. Cappelli. 2024. "Can Workplaces Have Too Much Psychological Safety?" *Harvard Business Review*. https://hbr.org/2024/01/can-workplaces-have-too-much-psychological-safety.

Erikson, T. 2021. *Surrounded by Bad Bosses (and Lazy Employees): How to Stop Struggling, Start Succeeding, and Deal with Idiots at Work*. St. Martin's Essentials.

Flint, D. 2018. *Think Beyond Value—Building Strategy to Win*. Morgan James Publishing.

Fuller, T. P. 2019. *Global Occupational Safety and Health Management Handbook*. Taylor & Francis Group.

Gentile, V. n.d. "20 Forward-Thinking Companies Offering B Corp Jobs That Matter." https://www.monster.com/career-advice/article/b-corporations.

Gilman, H., and K. Blumenthal. 1986. "Two Wal-Mart Officials Vie for Top Post." *The Wall Street Journal*, July 23, 6.

Glick, E. 1995. "Who Are They?" *Time*, May 1, 44–51.

Hagan, Phillip E., J. F. Montgomery, and J. T. O'Reilly. 2001. *Accident Prevention Manual*. National Safety Council.

Haws. n.d. "5 Safest Companies in-the United States." https://www.hawsco.com/blog/5-safest-companies-in-the-united-states/.

Helbig, K., and M. Norman. 2023. *Psychological Safety Playbook*. Page Two Press.

Hall, D. T. 1976. *Careers in Organizations*. Goodyear.

Hill, J. M. M., and E. L. Trist. 1953. "A Consideration of Industrial Accidents as a Means of Withdrawal from the Work Situation." *Human Relations* 6 (4), 357–380.

Howatt, B. 2024. "The Dark Side of the Psychological Health and Safety Conversation." *OHS Canada*. https://www.ohscanada.com/features/the-dark-side-of-the-psychological-health-and-safety-conversation/.

Howie, L. 2007. "The Terrorism Threat and Managing Workplaces." *Disaster Prevention and Management* 16 (1): 70–78.

Jansen, L. 2021. "The Danger of Psychological Safety." *LinkedIn*. https://www.linkedin.com/pulse/danger-psychological-safety-laura-jansen-she-her-/.

Johnson, P. 1986. "The Cancer of Terrorism." In *Terrorism*, edited by B. Netanyahu. Farrar, Straus Giroux.

Kelly, J. M. 1995. "Get a Grip on Stress." *HR Magazine*, February, 51–58.

Kets de Vries, M. F. R., and C. Rook. 2018. "Coaching Challenging Executives," In *Mastering Executive Coaching*, edited by J. Passmore and B. Underhill. Routledge. INSEAD Working Paper No. 2018/01/EFE.

Kiechel III, W. 1985. "The Importance of Being Visible." *Fortune*, June 24, 141–143.

Kinney, J. A. 1995. *Violence at Work*. Prentice-Hall.

Kozmetsky, R., and G. Kozmetsky. 1981. *Making It Together: A Survival Manual for the Executive Family*. Free Press.

Krantz, L., and T. Lee. 2015. *Jobs Rated Almanac: The Best Jobs and How to Get Them*. John Wiley & Sons.

Kuder, J. 2017. "Why Do People Have Accidents?" https://avatarms.com/accidents/.

Landy, F., J. C. Quick, and S. Kasl. 1994. "Work, Stress, and Well-Being." *International Journal of Stress Management* 1 (1): 33–73.

Laqueur, W. 1987. *The Age of Terrorism*. Little, Brown and Company.

Lyons, P. V. 1987. "EAPs: The Only Real Cure for Substance Abuse." *Management Review* 76 (3): 38–41.

Manuele, F. A. 2003. *On the Practice of Safety*. 3rd ed. Wiley-Interscience.

The Marketing Recruiter. 2025. "Staying Grounded in a Skyrocketing Job Market." https://www.themarketingrecruiter.com/2025/01/staying-grounded-in-a-skyrocketing-job-market.html.

Mascali, M. n.d. "Your Guide to New-Collar Jobs." https://www.monster.com/career-advice/article/new-collar-jobs-1216.

Maximo, N., M. W. Stander, and L. Coxen. 2019. "Authentic Leadership and Work Engagement: The Indirect Effects of Psychological Safety and Trust in Supervisors." *SA Journal of Industrial Psychology* 45 (1): 1–11.

Mauer, R. 2025. "Will the US Labor Market Rebound in 2025?" https://www.shrm.org/topics-tools/news/talent-acquisition/us-labor-market-rebound-2025.

Melhorn, S. F., and M. Hoover. 2025. "Understanding America's Labor Shortage: The Most Impacted Industries." https://www.uschamber.com/workforce/understanding-americas-labor-shortage-the-most-impacted-industries.

Michaud, P. A. 1995. *Accident Prevention and OSHA Compliance*. CRC Press, Inc.

Montana, C. 1986. "Career Couples Find Vacations Hard to Plan." *The Wall Street Journal*, August 4, A15.

Nater, F., D. D. Van Fleet, and E. W. Van Fleet. 2023. *Combating Workplace Violence: Creating and Maintaining Safe Work Environments*. Information Age Publishing.

National Institute for Occupational Safety and Health. 2002. *Worker Health Chartbook, 2000—Nonfatal Illness*. Department of Health and Human Services Centers for Disease Control and Prevention National Institute for Occupational Safety and Health.

Nichols, T. 1997. *The Sociology of Industrial Injury*. Mansell Publishing.

Patmore, A. 2006. *The Truth about Stress*. Atlantic Books.

Patrontasch, B. n.d. "Workplace Accident: A Comprehensive Guide." *https://www.myshyft.com/glossary/workplace-accident/*.

Payscale. n.d. "5 Jobs That Pay 80k+ Per Year Without a College Degree." https://www.payscale.com/career-advice/5-jobs-that-pay-80k-per-year-without-a-college-degree.

Powell, G. N., and L. A. Maniniero. 1992. "Cross Currents in the River of Time: Conceptualizing the Complexities of Women's Careers." *Journal of Management*, June 1, 215–237.

Rigby, A. 2024. "Psychological safety at work: Why your team really needs it." https://getmarlee.com/blog/psychological-safety.

Russell, A. M. 1989. "High-Tech Corporate Careers: Where Career Ladders Are Like Roller Coasters." *Working Woman*, May 1, 55–86.

Safety Leadership Conference, 2025. "Best Practices in Safety Leadership." https://www.safetyleadershipconference.com/2025/ASC24.

Savas, O. 2019. "Impact of Dysfunctional Leadership on Organizational Performance." *Global Journal of Management and Business Research* 19 (1): 37–41.

Schnitzer, K. 2021. "This Is What Work Will Look Like in 2030, and It Isn't Pretty." https://www.theladders.com/career-advice/this-is-what-work-will-look-like-in-2030-and-it-isnt-pretty?utm

Scotti, A. J. 1986. *Executive Safety and International Terrorism: A Guide for Travelers*. Prentice-Hall, Inc.

Serrette, S. 2001. "Planning and Organizing a Safety Program." *Occupational Health and Safety* 70 (7): 26–30.

Stackel. L. 1987. "EAPs in the Workplace." *Employment Relations Today* 14 (3): 289–294.

Staffing Industry Analysts. 2017. "Manpower Exec Says 65% of Tomorrow's Jobs Don't Exist Today (CNBC)." https://www.staffingindustry.com/news/global-daily-news/manpower-exec-says-65-tomorrows-jobs-dont-exist-today-cnbc#:~:text=Main%20content,create%20different%20kinds%20of%20jobs.

Taylor J., D. Collins, and M. Ashford. 2022. "Psychological Safety in High-Performance Sport: Contextually Applicable?" *Frontiers in Sports Active Living* 4: 823488. https://www.ncbi.nlm.nih.gov/pmc/articles/PMC9125081/.

The Muse Editors. 2024. "70 Smart Questions to Ask in an Interview in 2025." https://www.themuse.com/advice/51-interview-questions-you-should-be-asking.

Tolbert, T. 2025. "Navigating the 2025 Job Market: Challenges, Frustrations, and New Opportunities." https://www.linkedin.com/pulse/navigating-2025-job-market-challenges-frustrations-new-tasha-tolbert-0rwne/.

Unknown. 1989. "Winning Friends and Influencing People." *Hispanic Business*, July 1, 20–25.

Unknown. 1995. "Breaking Point." *Newsweek*, March 6, 56–62.

Unknown. 1995. "The Blood of Innocents." *Time*, May 1, 57–64.

Unknown. 1986. "Male vs. Female: What a Difference It Makes in Business Careers." *The Wall Street Journal*, December 9, 1.

U.S. Department of Labor. n.d. "Guidance and Tips for Employers." https://www.osha.gov/workplace-stress/employer-guidance; Anonymous. n.d. "Managing Work-Related Stress." https://www.urmc.rochester.edu/encyclopedia/content?contenttypeid=1&contentid=2882

Warner, J. 2014. "Fact Sheet: The Women's Leadership Gap." https://www.americanprogress.org/article/fact-sheet-the-womens-leadership-gap/#:~:text=A%20stalled%20revolution,increased%20more%20than%20six%2Dfold.

Valladares, M. R. 2025. "February 2025 Job Cuts Are the Highest Since Covid-19 Peak." https://www.forbes.com/sites/mayrarodriguezvalladares/2025/03/06/job-cuts-are-already-higher-than-all-of-2024/.

Van Der Loo, H., and J. Beks. 2020. *Praatkaarten Psychologische veiligheid*. Boom.

Van Fleet, D. D. 2024. *Dysfunctional Organizations*. Business Expert Press.

Van Fleet, D. D. 2025. *The Manager's Guide to Psychological Safety*. Business Expert Press.

Van Fleet, D. D., and E. W. Van Fleet. 2006. "Internal Terrorists: The Terrorists Inside Organizations." *Journal of Managerial Psychology* 21 (8): 763–774.

Van Fleet, D. D., and E. W. Van Fleet. 2007. "Preventing Workplace Violence: The Violence Volcano Metaphor." *Journal of Applied Management and Entrepreneurship* 12 (3): 17–36.

Van Fleet, D. D., and E. W. Van Fleet. 2010. *The Violence Volcano: Reducing the Threat of Workplace Violence*. Information Age Publishing.

Van Fleet, D. D., and E. W. Van Fleet. 2012. "Towards a Behavioral Description of Managerial Bullying." *Employee Responsibilities and Rights Journal* 24 (3): 197–215.

Van Fleet, D. D., and E. W. Van Fleet. 2022. *Bullying and Harassment at Work: An Innovative Approach to Understanding and Prevention*. Edward Elgar Publishing Inc.

Van Fleet, E. W., and D. D. Van Fleet. 1998. "Terrorism and the Workplace: Concepts and Recommendations." In *Dysfunctional Behavior in Organizations: Violent and Deviant Behavior*, edited by R. W. Griffin, A. O'Leary-Kelly, and J. Collins, vol. 23, part A. JAI Press.

Van Fleet, E. W., and D. D. Van Fleet. 2007. *Workplace Survival: Dealing with Bad Bosses, Bad Workers, Bad Jobs*. Publish America.

Van Fleet, E. W., and D. D. Van Fleet. 2014. *Violence at Work: What Everyone Should Know*. Information Age Publishing.

Vanta, B. 2023. "The Most Common Work-Related Injuries." https://facty.com/conditions/injury/the-most-common-work-related-injuries/?utm_.

Wang, C. C. K. 1993. *OSHA Compliance and Management Handbook*. Noyes Publications.

Weinstein, M. 2023. "How Much Psychological Safety Is Too Much?" *Training Day Blog*. https://trainingmag.com/how-much-psychological-safety-is-too-much/.

WikiFreedom. n.d.. "Encore Careers." https://www.freedomgpt.com/wiki/encore-careers.

Work It Daily. 2024. "2 Stories That Will Land You a Job in 2025." https://newsletter.workitdaily.com/p/2-stories-that-will-land-you-a-job-in-2025.

Yate, M. 2006. *Hiring the Best*. Adams Media.

Zielinski, D. 2020. "What Does the Tech Revolution Mean for HR?" *HR Magazine* 65 (4): 78–81.

Glossary

Everyone, especially managers, should be familiar with these terms. It might be useful to copy these for reference, especially in meetings or group discussions.

AA: Affirmative Action

Abjection: Separating of an individual from the group through statements of disgust

Absenteeism: Intentional or habitual absence from work

Abuse: Any action that intentionally harms or injures another person

Acceptable Use Policy (AUP): A policy that defines the responsibilities and appropriate behavior of computer and network users

Accommodation: Making special circumstances for someone

Accountability: Answerability for actions, decisions, and performance

Activate: To make active; cause to function or act

ADA: Americans with Disabilities

ADD: Administration on Developmental Disabilities

ADEA: Age Discrimination in Employment Act

AFAB and AMAB: Acronyms meaning "assigned female/male at birth" (also designated female/male at birth or female/male assigned at birth)

AFDC: Aid to Families with Dependent Children

Affect: An emotion that changes or influences what you do or think

Affirmative action: Plans of action undertaken by organizations to comply with human rights legislation by actively striving to recruit, hire, train, develop, and promote women and members of minority groups

Affirmed gender: The gender by which one wishes to be known

Age discrimination: Discrimination based on age

Agent: A person who acts for or in the place of another person

Aggressive: Pursuing one's aims and interests forcefully, sometimes unduly so

Aggressor: A person who says or does hurtful things

Aggrieved person: Someone who has been discriminated against in some way

Agreeableness: The tendency to get along with other people

AIDS: Acquired Immune Deficiency Syndrome

Ally: A Person who helps or stands up for someone who is being bullied or the target of prejudice

Ambiguous information: Information that can be interpreted in multiple and often conflicting ways

Anger-related incidents: sudden display of aggression, impulsivity, or disruptive behavior

Antibias: A commitment to avoid prejudice, stereotyping, and all forms of discrimination

Antisocial: Not sociable; not wanting the company of others

Anxiety: A feeling of worry, nervousness, or unease, typically about an imminent event or something with an uncertain outcome

Apology: A regretful acknowledgment of an offense

Arbitrator: A labor law specialist paid jointly by the union and the organization to listen to both sides of a labor dispute and then decide how the dispute should be settled

Assault and battery: The combination of two violent crimes—assault (the threat of violence) and battery (crime) (physical violence)

Assault: Intentionally putting someone in reasonable apprehension of an imminent harmful or offensive contact; physical injury is not required

Assessment center: An employee selection technique that allows human resource managers to observe and evaluate a prospective employee's performance on simulated tasks such as decision making and time management

Assets: Items of value owned by the company

At-will: An employee can be fired for any reason or for no reason at all

Attitudes: Predispositions to respond favorably or unfavorably to something

Attorney/client privilege: Communication made in confidence between a client and counsel for the purpose of seeking or providing legal counsel or advice

Avoidance: Actions a person takes to escape from difficult thoughts and feelings

Backpay: Money that an employer owes an employee for work that he or she did in the past

Basis: A basis is the "reason" being alleged for discrimination

Battery: The actual act that causes physical harm

Benchmarking: Comparing performance on specific dimensions with the performance of high-performing organizations

Benefits (fringe): Indirect compensation paid to employees, such as health care, life insurance, vacations, and sick leave

BFOQ: Bona Fide Occupational Qualification

Bias: A tendency to believe that some people, ideas, etc., are better than others, which usually results in treating some people unfairly

BJA: Bureau of Justice Assistance

BLS: Bureau of Labor Statistics

Bothering: Annoying or pestering someone

Bottom-up change: Change that is implemented gradually and involves managers and employees at all levels of an organization

Bullying: a form of workplace victimization consisting of repeated aggressive conduct, verbal abuse, or other acts of incivility that are humiliating, intimidating, isolating, or destabilizing and are intended to interfere with work and result in physical, professional, or psychological harm to an employee, including making the target feel threatened, vulnerable, and unable to define himself/herself against the recurring negative actions

Burnout: A state of emotional, physical, and mental exhaustion caused by excessive and prolonged stress

Bystander: A person who witnesses bias or other abusive behavior

Capital: Anything that confers value or benefit to its owners, such as its equipment or machinery, intellectual property like patents, financial assets, or its employees

Career counseling: Advice and assistance provided informally or formally to the individual regarding his career development and planning

Career development: A careful, systematic approach to assuring that sound career choices are made; involves both career planning (an individual element) and career management (an organizational element)

Career information systems: The combination of internal job markets with formal career counseling and the maintenance of a career information center for employees

Career management: The organizational element of career development, involving career counseling, career pathing, career resources planning, and career information systems

Career pathing: Identifying coherent progressions of jobs (tracks, routes, or paths) that are of particular interest to the organization

Career planning: Making detailed and specific decisions and plans about career goals and how to achieve them

Career plateau: A position from which the chances of being promoted or obtaining a more responsible job are slight

Career stages: Spans of years during which an individual has different types of concerns about job and career, sometimes labeled as the stages of career exploration, establishment, maintenance, and decline

Career: A sequence of attitudes and behaviors that a person perceives to be related to work experience during his or her life. The sum total of work-related experiences throughout a person's life.

CDC: U.S. Centers for Disease Control and Prevention

CEA: Council of Economic Advisers

Civil lawsuit: A court-based process through which Person A can seek to hold Person B liable for some type of harm or wrongful act

Climate: The social environment of the organization

CMS: Center for Management Services

Codes of conduct: Meaningful symbolic statements about the importance of adhering to high ethical standards in business

Coercion: Using power or force to impose an unwanted behavior

Cohesiveness: The extent to which group members are motivated to remain together

COLA: Cost of Living Adjustment

Coming out: Disclosing a lesbian, gay, bisexual, or transgender/gender-expansive identity within themselves first, and then choosing to reveal it to others

Compensation: Wages and salaries paid to employees for their services

Competitive advantage: The ability of one organization to outperform other organizations because it produces desired goods or services more efficiently and effectively than they do. The component of strategy that specifies the advantages that the organization holds relative to its competitors

Complainant: A person, group, or company that makes a complaint, as in a legal action (see also plaintiff)

Complaint: A complaint is an allegation of illegal discrimination

Compliance: Going along with the boss's request but without any stake in the result

Compromise: An agreement or a settlement of a dispute that is reached by each side making concessions

Conflict of interest: A situation where the employee's decision may be compromised because of competing loyalties

Conflict: Active disagreement between people with opposing opinions or principles

Constructive discharge: Conditions are so hostile that the target is forced to leave work

Corroborate: Person or information that confirms or gives support to a statement, theory, or finding

Credibility: Reputation as to believability

Crisis management team: A group assembled at the top of an organization to develop plans and actions to prevent workplace violence

Culture: Values and behaviors that contribute to the unique social and psychological environment of a business

Cyberbullying: Willful and repeated harm inflicted through the use of computers, cell phones, or other electronic devices

Damages: A remedy in the form of a monetary award to be paid to a claimant as compensation for loss or injury

Defaming: Making a false statement that injures someone's reputation or standing within a group

Defendant: A person, company, etc., against whom a claim or charge is brought in a court; person or entity being sued (see plaintiff)

Denigration: Sending or posting gossip or rumors about a person that damages that person's reputation or friendships

DHHS: Department of Health and Human Services

Discipline: Punishment inflicted by way of correction and training

Discovery: Obtaining and disclosing evidence and the position of each side of a case so that all parties involved can decide whether to move to trial or negotiate an early settlement

Discrimination: Unfair treatment of one person or group of people because of the person or group's identity (e.g., race, gender, ability, religion, culture, etc.)

Disparaging terms: Words used to degrade individual characteristics

Disparate impact: One group receives less favorable results than another

Disparate treatment: One group is subjected to inconsistent application of rules and policies relative to others

Disruptive: Behavior that causes difficulties that interrupt performance or prevent it from continuing

Diversity: Differences among people in age, gender, race, ethnicity, religion, sexual orientation, socioeconomic background, and capabilities/disabilities

DOC: Department of Commerce

DOE: Department of Energy

DOI: Department of Interior

DOJ: Department of Justice

DOL: Department of Labor

DOT: Department of Transportation

Downsizing: A reduction in organizational size and operating costs implemented by management in order to improve organizational efficiency, productivity, and/ or the competitiveness of the organization

Dual-career families: Households in which both the husband and the wife are pursuing careers, not merely earning an income

Dual-income families: Households in which both the husband and the wife earn a paycheck

Due diligence: Reasonable steps taken by a person in order to satisfy parties and to avoid harm to those involved

Dysfunctional organization: An organization that undermines the purpose, health, wholeness, safety, solidarity, and worth of an organization or its stakeholders

EBSA: Employee Benefits Security Administration

ECAB: Employees' Compensation Appeals Board

ED: Department of Education

EDA: Economic Development Administration

EEOC (Equal Employment Opportunity Commission): The agency responsible for enforcing federal laws regarding discrimination or harassment against job applicants or employees in the United States

Effectiveness: Doing the right things in the right way at the right times. A measure of the appropriateness of the goals an organization is pursuing and of the degree to which the organization achieves those goals.

Empathy: The ability to identify and share feelings with someone

Employment at will: Freedom of the organization to employ someone when it desires and therefore to dismiss the employee at any time for any reason

Empowerment: Expanding employees' tasks and responsibilities

Enabling factors: Those things that improve your ability to manage other abusive behavior

Enticement: Attracting by arousing hope or desire

EPA: Environmental Protection Agency or Equal Pay Act

Equality: Having the same or similar rights and opportunities as others

Equity: The quality of being fair or just

Eroding factors: Those things that impede your ability to reduce other abusive behavior

ESA: Employment Standards Administration; Economics and Statistics Administration

ETA: Employment and Training Administration

Ethical dilemma: A situation where the manager is faced with two or more conflicting ethical issues

Ethics: A moral philosophy or code of morals practiced by a person or group of people

Ethnic group: People who share a common religion, color, or national origin

Evade: To endeavor to set aside truth or to escape punishment

Evidence: The means by which any alleged matter is established or disproved

Exclusion: Intentionally excluding someone from a group or its activities

Fair labor practices: Equitable practices concerning hiring, wages, union relations, etc.

FDA: U.S. Food and Drug Administration

Feedback: Response from the receiver of a message to the sender of that message; for instance, telling the employee the results of his or her performance appraisal

Filtering: Withholding part of a message out of the belief that the receiver does not need, will not want the information, or intentionally deprives the receiver of important information

Financial redress: Compensation for injuries sustained; recovery or restitution for harm or injury; damages or equitable relief

FLRA: Federal Labor Relations Authority

FMCS: Federal Mediation and Conciliation Service

FMLA: Family and Medical Leave Act

Front pay: Money awarded for lost compensation during the period between judgment and reinstatement, or if reinstatement is not feasible, instead of reinstatement

Gender identity: One's deeply held core sense of being a girl/woman, boy/man, some of both, or neither

Glass ceiling: A metaphor alluding to the invisible barriers that prevent minorities and women from being promoted to top corporate positions

Gossiping: Spreading information, usually incorrect, about a person

Grievance: A written statement or complaint filed by an employee with the union concerning the employee's alleged mistreatment by the company

Group cohesiveness: The degree to which members are attracted or loyal to a group

Group decision making: Choosing among alternatives by teams, committees, or other types of groups rather than by one individual

Group norms: Shared guidelines or rules for behavior that most group members follow

Group: Two or more people who interact regularly to accomplish a common goal

Groupthink: A phenomenon that happens when the maintenance of cohesion and good feelings overwhelms the purpose of the group. A pattern of faulty and biased decision making occurs in groups whose members strive for agreement among themselves at the expense of accurately assessing information relevant to a decision.

Grudge: A feeling of ill will or resentment

Harassment: Making any profane or antagonizing remarks to attempt to annoy, anger, harass, and impede movement or any act involving nuisance phone calls, or annoying pranks

Harm: Physical or psychological damage or injury

Hazing: Imposing humiliating or painful tasks

HIPAA: Health Insurance Portability and Accountability Act

HIV: Human immunodeficiency virus

Hostile work environment: The workplace creates an environment that is difficult or uncomfortable for another person to work in, due to discrimination

HPV: Human papillomavirus

HRSA: Health Resources and Services Administration

Human resource management (HRM): Activities that managers engage in to attract and retain employees and to ensure that they perform at a high level and contribute to the accomplishment of organizational goals

Humiliation: To reduce an individual to a lower position in one's own eyes or others' eyes: to embarrass them or make them ashamed

ICE: Immigration and Customs Enforcement

Ignore: Refuse to take notice of or acknowledge; disregard intentionally

ILAB: Bureau of International Labor Affairs

ILO: International Labor Organization

Inconsistency: A communication problem that exists when a person sends conflicting messages

Inequality: An unfair situation when some individuals have more rights or better opportunities than others

Inequity: Lack of fairness

Informal organization: The overall pattern of influence and interaction defined by all the informal groups within an organization. The system of behavioral rules and norms that emerge in a group.

Initiative: The ability to act on one's own, without direction from a superior

Injunction: A court order requiring a person to do or cease doing a specific action

Injustice: A situation in which the rights of a person or a group of people are ignored, disrespected, or discriminated against

Innuendo: An indirect derogatory statement

Intention: Something that you want and plan to do

Internal terrorism: Behavior that involves the intent to evoke fear or extreme stress to bring about a change that benefits the perpetrator

Interpersonal communication: Communication between people, especially small numbers of people, either orally, in writing, or nonverbally

Intimidation: Making others afraid or fearful through threatening behavior

Involvement: Taking part in something

IRS: Internal Revenue Service

Jealousy: Feeling or showing envy of someone or their achievements and advantages

LGBTQ: An acronym that collectively refers to individuals who are lesbian, gay, bisexual, transgender, or queer. It is sometimes stated as LGBT (lesbian, gay, bisexual, and transgender) or GLBT (gay, lesbian, bi, and transgender).

Life stress: Events or experiences that produce severe strain, for example, bullying or harassment on the job

Litigation: The process of resolving disputes by filing or answering a complaint through the court system

Longevity: Suggests how long any given effort to deal with other abusive behavior might be sustained

MBDA: Minority Business Development Agency

Mediation: A process wherein the parties meet with a mutually selected impartial and neutral person who assists them in the negotiation of their differences

Mentor: An experienced and trusted adviser

Merit Systems Protection Board (MSPB): Federal agency responsible for dealing with personnel actions and appeals

Micromanage: Managers who cannot turn over a worker's job to the worker. They feel a need to tell the worker usually in minute detail how to perform a particular job, and then they still stay in control every step of the way.

Minority: A smaller group within a state, region, or country differs in race, religion, or national origin from the dominant group

Molestation: Sexual assault or abuse of a person, especially a woman or child

Molesting: Assault or abuse (a person, especially a woman) sexually

Name-calling: The use of words to hurt, belittle, or be mean to someone or a group

Negotiation: A method of conflict resolution in which the parties in conflict consider various alternative ways to allocate resources to each other in order to come up with a solution acceptable to them all

Negotiator: The role that a manager plays when attempting to work out agreements and contracts that operate in the best interests of the organization

Networking: The exchange of information through a group or network of interlinked computers

NIH: National Institutes of Health

NIJ: National Institute of Justice

NIOSH: National Institute for Occupational Safety and Health

NIOSH: The National Institute for Occupational Safety and Health is part of the CDC charged with developing new knowledge in the field of occupational safety and health and transferring that knowledge into practice

NLRB: National Labor Relations Board

NMB: National Mediation Board

Nonverbal communication: Gestures and facial expressions, which do not involve speaking but can also include nonverbal aspects of speech (tone and volume of voice, etc.)

Norm: A standard of behavior that the group develops for its members

Normality: The condition or state of being usual, typical, or expected (normal)

OBL: Office of Business Liaison

Occupational crime: Offenses that are committed by someone during the course of his or her employment

Occupational deviant behavior: Self-serving deviant acts that occur at the workplace

OCR: Office for Civil Rights

Offense: A perceived insult to or disregard for an individual

OLMS: Office of Labor-Management Standards

On notice: Has received a notification so that one cannot claim to be unaware of a situation

OPM: Office of Personnel Management

Organizational culture: Values and behaviors that contribute to the unique social and psychological environment of a business

Organizational environment: The set of forces and conditions that operate beyond an organization's boundaries but affect a manager's ability to acquire and utilize resources

Organizational politics: Activities that individuals engage in to increase their power and to use power effectively to achieve their goals and overcome resistance or opposition

OSBP: Office of Small Business Programs

OSDBU: Office of Small and Disadvantaged Business Utilization

OSHA: Occupational Safety and Health Administration is charged with ensuring safe and healthful working conditions for workers by setting and enforcing standards and by providing training, outreach, education, and assistance

Outplacement: Support service provided by some organizations to help former employees transition to new jobs

Overt discrimination: Knowingly and willingly denying diverse individuals access to opportunities and outcomes in an organization

OVW: Office on Violence Against Women

OWBO: Office of Women's Business Ownership

OWCP: Office of Workers' Compensation Programs

Pain and suffering: The physical or emotional distress resulting from an injury

Participative management: Giving employees a voice in how things are done in organizations

Perception: The recognition and interpretation of sensory information

Perpetrator: A person who engages in unacceptable behavior or who carries out a harmful, illegal, or immoral act

Personal injury: Physical injury inflicted on a person, as opposed to damage to property or reputation

Plaintiff: A person or entity filing a lawsuit (see Defendant)

Positive approaches: Methods that stress prevention and support rather than punishment

Power imbalance: A situation where one person or group has an advantage over others

Power: An individual's ability to control or direct others

Predispositions: The tendency to perceive or act in a certain way because of previous experiences in one's background or environment

Prejudice: Judging or having an idea about someone or a group of people before you actually know them

Prima facie: Latin for "on first view" or "at first appearance." In EEO cases, complainants present evidence and arguments to support a claim of discrimination

Professional ethics: Standards that govern how members of a profession are to make decisions when the way they should behave is not clear-cut

Protected class: Groups protected from employment discrimination by law

Psychological trauma: An emotional response to a terrible event like an accident, rape, or natural disaster. Immediately after the event, shock and denial are typical (www.apa.com).

Public apology: Apologizing in the presence of others

Punishment: Administering an undesired or negative consequence when dysfunctional behavior occurs; reprimands, discipline, fines, etc. that are used to shape behavior by causing a reduction in unwanted behaviors

Punitive damages: Damages assessed in the legal process to punish a defendant and to prevent him or her from hurting others by the same or similar actions

Quid pro quo: A manager or other authority figure offers or merely hints that he or she will give the employee something (a raise or a promotion) in return for that employee's satisfaction of a sexual demand

Racism: Prejudice and/or discrimination against people because of their racial group

Rareness: The capability of managing the contributing factors to other abusive behavior within the organization

Reasonable person standard: A test in personal injury cases that jurors use to determine if a defendant acted like other people would have in the same situation

Recruiting: The process of attracting a pool of qualified applicants who are interested in working for the company

Redress: The setting right of what is wrong

Remedies: A form of court enforcement of a legal right resulting from a successful civil lawsuit

Resistance: The negative, uncooperative response of persons when their boss attempts to influence them

Retaliation: An employer punishes an employee for engaging in legally protected activity

Rumors: Unofficial pieces of information of interest to organizational members but with no identifiable source

Sabotage: Acting to deliberately destroy, damage, or obstruct (something), especially in retaliation

SBA: Small Business Administration

SEC: Securities and Exchange Commission

Self-efficacy: Your belief in your own abilities to deal with various situations

Sexting: Sending sexually explicit photographs or messages via mobile phone or other electronic means

Sexual harassment: Unwelcome sexual advances, requests for sexual favors, or other verbal or physical conduct of a sexual nature

Shunning: An act of social rejection or emotional distancing

Smoothing: Downplaying the importance of a problem

Stalking: Following someone stealthily to cause them fear

Stereotype: False idea that all group members are the same and/or think and behave in the same way

Stress: A feeling of emotional strain and pressure

Strict liability: Imposes legal responsibility for damages or injuries even if the person who was found strictly liable did not act with fault or negligence

Tagout: disabling machinery so it cannot be used

Target: Someone who is subject to other abusive behavior or treated in hurtful ways by a person or a group on purpose and over and over

Team building: A series of activities and exercises designed to enhance the motivation and satisfaction of people in groups by fostering mutual understanding, acceptance, and group cohesion

Team: A group whose members work intensely with each other to achieve a specific, common goal or objective

Terror: Violence or threats of violence used for intimidation or coercion

Terrorism: Intimidation or coercion by instilling fear

Third-party harassment: Harassment by someone who is not a member of the organization (e.g., customer, supplier)

Threat: The implication or expression of intent to inflict physical harm or actions that a reasonable person would interpret as a threat to physical safety or property

Title VII: Part of the Civil Rights Act of 1964 is a federal law that protects employees against discrimination based on certain specified characteristics: race, color, national origin, sex, and religion

Tolerance: The willingness to accept opinions, behaviors, and characteristics different from one's own

Traits: Characteristics of a person

Transgender: The term for people whose gender identity differs from that assigned at birth (e.g., assigned girl or boy)

Turnover: The number or percentage of workers who leave an organization and are replaced by new employees

Union: an organization formed by workers who join together and use their strength to have a voice in their workplace

Unwelcome conduct: Any behavior by subordinates, peers, or superiors that is deemed offensive or unwelcome by an employee

USDA: U.S. Department of Agriculture

Value: The organization's productivity and its value to customers, clients, and employees

Vengeance: Infliction of injury, harm, humiliation, or the like, on a person by another who has been harmed by that person

Verbal abuse: Making profane or antagonizing remarks in an attempt to annoy anger or harass

V-REEL®: Framework, originally developed for strategic analysis in organizations (Flint, 2018), provides a unique way of thinking about the causes of other abusive behavior and how to eradicate it. It consists of five components—Value, Rareness, Eroding factors, Enabling factors, and Longevity

Vulnerable individuals: Those who are or may be for any reason unable to take care of themselves, or unable to protect themselves against significant harm or exploitation

Whistleblower: A person who reports illegal or unethical behavior

Withdrawal: Avoiding people and activities you would usually enjoy; social isolation

Workplace violence: Behavior in which an employee, former employee, visitor, or service provider to a workplace inflicts or threatens serious harm, injury, or death to others at the workplace or inflicts damage to property. This behavior is pertinent in workplaces as defined as an official workplace or company-sponsored event.

Zero tolerance: A standard that establishes that any behavior, implied or actual, that violates the policy will not be tolerated

About the Author

David D. Van Fleet is Professor Emeritus at Arizona State University. He has over 50 years of experience in the practice, teaching, and research of management and organizations. He has taught at the University of Tennessee, the University of Akron, Texas A&M University, and Arizona State University, where he covered courses in human relations management, organizational behavior, management, and leadership. He draws upon this impressive career to provide examples, analyses, and recommendations for dealing with dysfunctional organizations.

He has published over 100 journal articles or book chapters, including "What Members Need in Work Situations: Two Samples of Essential Managerial Leadership Behaviors" (*Journal of Managerial Issues*, 2022); "Baseballs or Cricket Balls: On the Meanings of Bullying and Harassment" (*Journal of Human Resource and Sustainability Studies*, 2018); "Future Challenges and Issues of Bullying in the Workplace" in Laura M. Crothers and John Lipinski (eds.), *Bullying in the Workplace: Causes, Symptoms, and Remedies*. 2014, Taylor & Francis; "Towards a Behavioral Description of Managerial Bullying" (*Employee Responsibilities and Rights Journal*, 2012); "Preventing Workplace Violence: The Violence Volcano Metaphor" (*Journal of Applied Management and Entrepreneurship*, 2007); "Internal Terrorists: The Terrorists Inside Organizations" (*Journal of Managerial Psychology*, 2006); "Terrorism and the Workplace: Concepts and Recommendations" in *Dysfunctional Behavior in Organizations* (JAI Press, 1998); "Terrorism and the Workplace: Concepts and Recommendations" in R. W. Griffin, A. O'Leary-Kelly, and J. Collins (eds.), *Dysfunctional Behavior in Organizations: Violent and Deviant Behavior*. 1998, 23, Part a. JAI Press; and "Workplace Violence: Moving Toward Minimizing Risks" (Project Minerva publication, funded by OSHA, 1996).

The following are the list of books he has published:

Van Fleet, D. D. 2025. *The Manager's Guide to Psychological Safety*. Business Expert Press.

Van Fleet. D. D. 2024. *Ella's Songs*. Pine Book Writing, Richmond Hill, ON L4C 3B2, Canada.

Van Fleet. D. D. 2024. *Ella's Life*. Copyright by the author. ISBN-13 979-8302777829.

Van Fleet, D. D. 2024. *Dysfunctional Organizations*. Business Expert Press.

Nater, F., Van Fleet, D. D., and E. W. Van Fleet. 2023. *Combating Workplace Violence: Creating and Maintaining Safe Work Environments*. Information Age Publishing.

Van Fleet, D. D., and E. W. Van Fleet. 2022. *Bullying and Harassment at Work: An Innovative Approach to Understanding and Prevention*. Edward Elgar Publishing.

Van Fleet, D. D. 2020. *Quality Time: Productivity Through Time Management*. Information Age Publishing.

Van Fleet, E. W., and D. D. Van Fleet. 2014. *Violence at Work: What Everyone Should Know*. Information Age Publishing.

Van Fleet, D. D., E. W. Van Fleet, and G. J. Seperich. 2014. *Agribusiness: Principles of Management*. Delmar/Cengage Learning.

Griffin, R. W., and D. D. Van Fleet. 2013. *Management Skills: Assessment and Development*. SouthWestern/Cengage Learning.

Van Fleet, D. D., and E. W. Van Fleet. 2010. *The Violence Volcano: Reducing the Threat of Workplace Violence*. Information Age Publishing.

Van Fleet, E. W., and D. D. Van Fleet. 2007. *Workplace Survival: Dealing with Bad Bosses, Bad Workers, Bad Jobs*. Publish America.

Van Fleet, D. D., and T. O. Peterson. 1994. *Contemporary Management*. 3rd ed. Houghton Mifflin, in collaboration with R. W. Griffin.

Van Fleet, D. D. 1991. *Behavior in Organizations*. Houghton Mifflin, in collaboration with G. Moorhead and R. W. Griffin.

Van Fleet, D. D. 1991. *Contemporary Management*. 2nd ed. Houghton Mifflin, in collaboration with R. W. Griffin.

Van Fleet, D. D. 1988. *Contemporary Management*. 1st ed. Houghton Mifflin.

Van Fleet, D. D., and G. A. Yukl. *Military Leadership: An Organizational Behavior Perspective.* JAI Press, Inc., 1986.

Albanese, R., and D. D. Van Fleet. 1983. *Organizational Behavior: A Managerial Viewpoint.* Dryden.

Afterword

When the book was finished, David celebrated at his favorite restaurant. He relaxed, enjoyed the company of his son, and partook of a novel beverage.

Index

www.ingramcontent.com/pod-product-compliance
Lightning Source LLC
Chambersburg PA
CBHW061316220326
41599CB00026B/4903